Language
Education
in the
Caribbean

Dennis Craig, by Philbert Gajadhar

Language Education in the Caribbean

Selected Articles by Dennis Craig

EDITED BY **JEANNETTE ALLSOPP** AND **ZELLYNNE JENNINGS**

THE UNIVERSITY OF THE WEST INDIES PRESS

Jamaica • Barbados • Trinidad and Tobago

The University of the West Indies Press
7A Gibraltar Hall Road, Mona
Kingston 7, Jamaica
www.uwipress.com

A catalogue record of this book is available from the National Library of Jamaica.

978-976-640-497-0 (print)
978-976-640-536-6 (Kindle)
978-976-640-540-3 (ePub)

Cover design by Robert Harris
Typesetting by The Beget, India
Printed in the United States of America

Contents

Foreword

The Thoughts of a "Rip Van Winkle"?

> There is no fundamental reason why, within discrete societies and ultimately the world at large, human beings cannot see themselves first as human beings, with a unity that transcends the biological superficiality of race, and the cultural specifics such as language, religion, class and so on, that mankind has inherited different parts of the world
>
> – Dennis Craig, *Viewpoint*,
> Guyana Broadcasting Company,
> 23 September 1991

In addition to his prodigious output on the issues of language learning and teaching in English–based Creole-speaking Caribbean societies, Dennis was equally concerned with the nature of their social systems and the issues arising from their impact on education in general. To this end, he started writing for the Guyana Broadcasting Company in 1989, as he was then based in Guyana, but the kinds of problems that he treated were comparable to those also being experienced by other states in the Caribbean Community (CARICOM).

When he became vice chancellor of the University of Guyana in 1991, he gave up doing *Viewpoint* so as to concentrate on the demands of his new job. What he thought at the time was his last *Viewpoint* (7 October 1991) he titled "The Thoughts of Rip Van Winkle". Seven months later he resumed the viewpoints because he found it impossible to divorce issues in higher education from the local issues that intrude into the business of the university and "that beg for the public expression of rational opinion". He also spoke of the need to confront certain mentalities in the society such as those who believe "that the solution to the world's problems lies in the distribution, not the increased production of wealth;

that we must level everything and make all things, including salaries, equal for everybody". For his outspokenness, Dennis's viewpoints were described by some as "controversial" and because he spoke on state radio they were viewed as "politically biased". But which opinion can escape either criticism?

Dennis saw himself as a Caribbean man. He owed many of his accomplishments to his adopted country – Jamaica – where he lived for most of his life and where he chose to die. Jamaica had a special place in his heart. But he loved the country of his birth in a way that a child loves a parent. His concern was always for the welfare of Guyana.

In 1990 the State Paper on Educational Policy had been announced and he was concerned with the implementation of what he termed "far-off dreams" embodied in the goals of the policy. In fact, in his viewpoint on 1 June 1990 he wrote on thoughts on "the dream paper", as the policy document had been dubbed by Ian McDonald. He felt there was a need to move the policy paper from rhetoric to reality by first identifying those goals that the education system could start working on immediately, as opposed to those that would first require an economic recovery.

In-service Training of Teachers and Principals

In August 1990 he was still preoccupied with that theme. He was concerned with how the country could move from the reality of the decline in the education system to the ideal envisaged given that the ideal depended on external funding. Since external funding usually took a long time to materialize, he urged the need to commence the rehabilitation of the education system by using existing resources. At the time, Dennis was the director of the National Centre for Educational Resource Development (NCERD). He did five viewpoints on ongoing activities in education at NCERD designed to help the rehabilitation of the education system using existing resources. The first viewpoint dealt with a workshop held in Kamarang, situated in the interior of Guyana in the Upper Mazaruni area, while the second focused on some factors to take into consideration while implementing the State Paper on Educational Policy. The third and fourth viewpoints dealt with NCERD's attempt to respond to the needs of children who were not successful at the secondary school entrance examination and ended up in community high schools. Issues relating to improving secondary education were also discussed. The final viewpoint dealt with provision in teacher training to ensure the continuous growth and professional development of the teacher.

At the time of the first workshop, he was leading the NCERD officers on a visit to Kamarang in the Upper Mazaruni in Region 7. This region is largely inhabited by Amerindians belonging to the Akawaio tribe. In meetings with the NCERD officers, they expressed concern over the fact that their children, whose indigenous language was Akawaio, were exposed to a centralized curriculum designed for speakers of standard Guyanese English Creole. Irregular patterns of attendance and using a curriculum designed for monogrades in the multi-grade situations which predominated in the region impacted negatively on the progress and achievement of the Amerindian children.

Dennis was cognizant of the fact that the workshop at Kamarang could not address all of these concerns. For example, teacher training in Guyana had never been designed to prepare teachers to function in situations where they can teach Amerindian children using their indigenous language. However, the workshop did focus on improving skills in multigrade teaching and on the use of the *Skills Reinforcement Curriculum Guides* to teach language arts more effectively. That was consistent with the existing resources at NCERD. The workshop at Kamarang was repeated in the remaining nine regions in the country.

The entire workshop targeted heads of schools and senior teachers who were then expected to return to their schools to train their teachers. The effect of the training was to be seen in improvement in literacy skills. In order to determine if such an improvement was taking place, the heads of schools were asked to send samples of the children's writing at specific times during the school year. The samples of writing were then analysed to enable a mapping of progress throughout the school year. The plan was to report back to the schools on their progress at a repeat of the workshop one year later.

Targeting of heads of schools for the workshops was done deliberately, as Dennis believed that school leaders should be instructional leaders first and administrators "incidentally". The "far-off dreams" of policy, he maintained, could not be achieved unless teachers' salaries were improved to deter them from migrating to greener pastures and also in an effort to attract bright young people to seeing teaching as their chosen profession. A willingness to accept new ideas and innovative teaching methodologies, he felt, were essential in order to halt the decline in education. Instead of school leaders, including education officers, just inspecting schools and reporting, they needed to engage the teachers in the schools and help them deal with the problems they faced in the classroom. Interestingly, the NCERD strategy won one of the Nessim Habif awards from the Caribbean Network for Educational Innovation and Development in 1989.

Primary and Secondary Education

In his third viewpoint, Dennis described NCERD's approach to curriculum development. He explained how NCERD had revised the curriculum guides for grades 7 to 9 designed for the community high schools. The teachers in these schools were given the drafts of the guides and provided with a form on which to report any difficulties and concerns they had in the use of the guides. The NCERD staff used the feedback to inform their revision of the guides. An underlying concern was how to provide the community high schools students with an opportunity to do subjects in the Caribbean Secondary Education Certificate like their peers in the more prestigious secondary high schools. Using improved teaching methods in the community high schools as used in the more prestigious schools was considered a positive move.

Dennis turned his attention to issues related to improving secondary education in his fourth viewpoint. He focused on the cost of textbooks and the attempt to reduce costs through the use of a book rental scheme. As a result of the latter the parent only had to find about one third of the cost of all the books that the child needed. The inability to address the aesthetics, physical education and craft as well as prevocational areas was also highlighted as a weakness of the existing curriculum.

Dennis returned to the issue of teacher training in his final viewpoint on education. Initial training, he underscored, must provide a sound foundation for the teacher, but provision must also be made for the ongoing training of the teacher. NCERD therefore had a role to play in this regard. Final-year students at the Cyril Potter College of Education attended seminars at NCERD to be introduced to the revised guides and new methodologies. Dennis also described the setting up of a technical committee of the advisory board of the Faculty of Education at the University of Guyana. This committee comprised the senior officers of the Ministry of Education, the director of NCERD, the dean and senior members of the Faculty of Education. The committee undertook the revision of the bachelor's and master's degree programmes. This resulted in the introduction of specializations in the Bachelor of Education degree at the nursery and primary levels as well as the strengthening of the content in the secondary specialization to enable teaching in the upper forms of the secondary school.

On 19 July 1992 Dennis wrote on the joys experienced by those students who passed the Common Entrance Examination and were fortunate to proceed to the prestigious secondary schools. Most of these are destined to pass the Caribbean Secondary Education Certificate examinations. He bemoaned the fate of those who failed the Common Entrance Examination and ended up in the "primary schools with tops". These schools catered to children between the ages of six to fourteen plus. For the most part they followed an advanced primary curriculum. These schools are known as "all-age" in other parts of the Caribbean. Dennis pointed to the report of the CARICOM Task Force on Education which was presented to ministers of education in May 1992. The report highlighted similar problems in the region as applied in Guyana, namely: the poor quality of literacy and numeracy skills at the primary level and the impact that this has on the secondary level. Education officials pointed out that the solutions to these problems were discussed as far back as the 1970s but few of them had been systematically carried out. Dennis decried the "surprising lack of continuity in the programmes of the Ministries of Education throughout the region".

Tertiary Education

Thoughts arising from the McIntyre and Bourne reports were the subject of his viewpoint on 19 March 1990. The viewpoint on 2 April 1990 referred to recommendations on education from the McIntyre and Bourne reports, both of which stressed the importance of tertiary level education. Dennis's concern was how to increase both the quantity and the quality of tertiary level education. He stated clearly his distress over the fact that the achievement of such goals is stymied by the low human inputs that are expected to contribute to the expansion of tertiary level institutions, but clearly cannot do so. The tertiary level institutions cannot recruit suitably qualified staff and there are few students adequately prepared to benefit from tertiary education. He urged the governments to start with improvements at the primary level so as to provide a surer foundation for secondary education which in turn would become a stronger recruiting ground for universities.

On 15 November 1993 Dennis returned to the theme of education; this time to the complaints about university graduates and their deficiency in general education characteristics, such as the roughness of their speech and their inability "to put two sentences together". But these are the very complaints, Dennis said, that are levelled against school-leavers, including those from the best secondary schools. Teachers at this level blame the deficiency on weaknesses at the primary level. Dennis traced the deficiencies in the education system to broad and general societal changes which had taken place over the past sixty years. These included the rapid democratization of education that had taken place in the postcolonial era which had given access to secondary education to children in the lower socio-economic classes and with them came cultural habits "including language that was once frowned upon and suppressed in traditional middle and upper class society". Non-standard speech (that is, Guyanese Creolese) became accepted as a legitimate form of language not to be treated as "bad language". At the same time, Dennis added, a grammar approach to English teaching went out of fashion and has not been replaced by the adapted second-language approach that should have replaced it. He concluded: "Do not express shock therefore that secondary schools and the University are affected. If our graduates had been taught to write Creolese, they would write you much better reports in Creolese than they can now write in English."

The University of Guyana

When he returned to the theme of the university in the 1992–93 academic year, in one viewpoint he highlighted the achievements of the University of Guyana since it opted out of the University of the West Indies in 1963: "Graduates of the University of Guyana can now be found in top management positions all over Guyana, in the Caribbean, and farther afield." However, the economic decline in the country had impacted negatively on the university, resulting in a deterioration of its physical infrastructure, inadequate funding, and staff so poorly paid that it had become impossible to attract and retain highly qualified staff. Some were of the view that the survival of the academic viability of the University of Guyana rested in a reintegration with the University of the West Indies. While not supporting this proposal, Dennis urged "inter-linkages between all tertiary institutions in the Region: complementary programmes, common courses and so on". The region, Dennis maintained, is much too small to sustain a multiplicity of totally unrelated tertiary institutions.

In August 1993 Dennis did several viewpoints on the University of Guyana. On 9 August he wrote about the abandonment of cost efficiency at the university as evidenced by the low student: staff ratios. Inadequate funding by the government accounted to some extent for the university not having the same staff: student ratios as economically run universities. Dennis, however, was able to report that for the first time in its thirty-year history, the university had enrolled three thousand students and the student: staff ratio had increased to

12.9 to 1. Furthermore the average cost per student had decreased from US$858 to US$653 (December 1992), but "low student costs at UG are being made possible almost exclusively by the sacrifice of UG academic staff".

His viewpoint of 23 August 1993 referred to unreasonable demands being made of the University of Guyana by the government in expecting large numbers of graduates in science and technology. The market for those specializations in the society is absent, he maintained, and the schools did not provide the foundation in mathematics and science to produce students who could enter the Faculties of Natural Sciences and Technology. "The University therefore is a part of a very vicious circle in educational development and it cannot break out of that circle on its own," he said.

In another viewpoint, Dennis's focus was on how the University of Guyana (with a population of three thousand) could move from accommodating just 3 per cent of its adult population (compared to 15 to 20 per cent in developed countries) to match the 40 per cent of their adult population which developed countries wanted to attain by 2000. The most feasible way of increasing the university population, Dennis maintained, was to "eliminate irrational requirements for entry to university programme" since "many traditional regulations governing entry to higher education are merely elitist barriers which have nothing to do with possession of intellect". He argued that students should be allowed to register for external studies, to develop the open learning concept so well exploited by universities in India, "and to exploit the full possibilities of distance education". Under his term as vice chancellor, the University of Guyana had already taken steps to move in these directions. Massive funding of the university, he felt, was necessary and students should be admitted without having to pay their costs while studying. They should repay the cost of their university education, after graduation.

As vice chancellor of the university, Dennis considered it necessary for the university to attain some measure of independence from a total reliance on government funding. On 12 March 1993 the private sector turned out in large numbers at the fund-raising dinner held to launch the university's thirty-fifth fund-raising drive. On 15 March, Dennis made mention of an encounter he had had with a banker friend who had pointed out that support from the private sector may be a "two-edged sword" for the university: providing financial support but at the same time taking greater interest in the business of the university. Was this desirable for an institution that valued its academic freedom? Dennis's response was that while universities should strongly resist any attempt at outside interference with their standards, their systems of appointing and promoting staff, and their systems of admitting, teaching, assessing and graduating students, the whole functioning of universities as institutions must be governed by accountability. The two edged sword the banker friend spoke of is not in reality a sword, Dennis maintained. "It is merely the healthy pressure of a modern society which no proper institution should seek to escape."

Human Relationships

In his viewpoint of 27 February 1989, Dennis noted the lack of concern or care for people, especially those in the lower-income bracket who have to queue for hours to purchase scarce goods. He issued a plea for extension of courtesy and care to the waiting public: "And such demonstrations of caring among us would go far towards softening the harshness of the socio-economic conditions that affect our society."

He returned to the theme in the viewpoint "on the powerful and the powerless" (10 December 1990) in which he referred to the turmoil into which Mr. Gorbachev's attempt to introduce an open and economically restructured social system have thrown the Soviet Union and Eastern Europe. What we are witnessing, Dennis argued, is the restoration of the primacy of the ordinary man and woman in that part of the world. He added: "Many of the violent eruptions that have followed the Restoration: physical assaults on communist parties, violent outbursts by racial minority groups . . . mostly stem from deep seated resentments of how officialdom has treated people." He urged the leaders in Guyana to learn from the experiences of the Soviet Union and Eastern Europe and remove the blockages to the smooth conduct of the daily life of the ordinary man and woman.

In October 1992, following a change of government, there was a call for national unity. In April 1990 Dennis had originally highlighted the theme of "bureaucracy and the ordinary citizen" whereby many people who are supposed to "serve the public" do not realize that the convenience of the ordinary citizen comes first and that the ordinary citizen is the ultimate boss. He then went on to highlight the human tendency of individuals to remove themselves from blame or prejudice which they readily perceive others to have and the hostile ways in which people treat each other. He wrote: "You have only to observe the roughness, the unfriendly, impolite and often uncivilized attitudes, the lack of caring that often confront the poor and ordinary citizen in some transaction or other of public business in our offices, our shops and stores, in the varied means of our transportation system, in chance encounters with officialdom you have only to observe these things in order to recognize the hangovers of colonial traditions."

Other themes that Dennis explored included the significance of independence. On the celebration of the twenty-fifth anniversary of Guyana's independence, he underscored the fact that independence "requires that we become identified as separate and distinct: a national group". He felt that this is particularly challenging for many. He wrote: "The phenomenon of living in one's native country but yet belonging elsewhere culturally and in one's perception is a common one today. It takes some intelligence, some individualism and some personal integrity today for one to remain distinctive and true to one's native identity. The industrialized world exerts a constant pressure on the mind to turn each of us into a replica of the anonymous, indistinguishable western north-Atlantic person."

Persistent attitudes was the subject of his viewpoint on 7 January 1991. Examples of these are: the prevalence of the "next week" syndrome, the tendency to defer anything that can be deferred, an avoidance of decision-making-resulting in an endless "passing of the buck". His viewpoint of 3 August 1992 reads like an ode to emancipation in which he urged listeners to recognize the impact of two hundred years of slavery as 'an agent of change' through which those who were emancipated captured an opportunity to assert their identity "already forged and sculpted deep within them by two hundred years of unique hardship, struggle and suffering". He ended that viewpoint by saying "today we celebrate the emergence of the Afro-Guyanese ones of us. May the libations we pour be plentiful, and may they safeguard our future as much as they honour our ancestors."

Among his favourite themes in his viewpoints were democracy and the wider applications of the principle that the customer is always right; historical and contemporary lessons towards tolerance and harmony in a multi-ethnic society; the futility of dwelling on the past, rather than realistically assessing the present and taking firm steps towards building the future, "a viewpoint that got me accused of being a Rip Van Winkle" (1 October 1991). "Now if my treatment of these themes and topics appears to be politically biased," wrote Dennis, "then so be it. Which thinking person can produce a body of ideas that subsequently cannot be analysed and classified under some political label or other? And we need more thinking people among us."

Conclusion

In conclusion, Dennis himself summed up his main concerns in his viewpoints: "I have tried to express in them more than anything else my concern that, as the economy of the country improves, our bureaucratic processes and ways of treating one another should also improve and that the interest and convenience of the ordinary person should always be put first."

Many of Dennis' viewpoints give us a blueprint for sound educational practices and if those are followed, they lead to a thinking society. Dennis was the consummate "thinking person". In his poem "Words", he writes, "After ten score years I hold a pen in a brown hand – which brings us back to words." He had the gift of words which he transformed into creations that have long outlived him. In his poem "Not Here to Stay", Dennis wrote "Some people are made so that they may stay no matter what you do; / very often they are women, sometimes men too."

This book is in honour of a man whom his great friend and colleague, Richard Allsopp, described in his eulogy as having lived a "quietly brilliant life". It is a testimony to a man who is here to stay, a man whose creative imagination manifested itself in an invaluable contribution to academia, the social and political arena and the aesthetics. He, like flowers, in his poem of the same name, "came stark glory like lightning in the dark".

Zellynne Jennings

Acknowledgements

We are grateful for permission to reprint from the original publishers of the articles by Dennis Craig as cited below. The articles have been reprinted as originally published, with minor updates to language usage (e.g., West Indies -> Caribbean; Anglophone -> English-speaking, English-official):

"Education and Creole English in the West Indies: Some Sociolinguistic Factors", in *Pidginization and Creolization of Language*, edited by Dell Hymes (Cambridge: Cambridge University Press, 1971).

"Reading and the Creole Speaker", *Torch: Journal of the Ministry of Education* (Jamaica) 22, no. 2 (1973).

"Bidialectal Education: Creole and Standard in the West Indies", *International Journal of the Sociology of Language* 8 (1976), reprinted in *Sociolinguistic Aspects of Language Learning and Teaching*, edited by J.B. Pride (Oxford: Oxford University Press, 1979).

"Creole and Standard: Partial Learning, Base Grammar and the Mesolect", in *Papers from the Twenty-ninth Annual Round Table Meeting in Languages and Linguistics. Georgetown University*, edited by J. Alatis (Washington, DC: Georgetown University Press, 1978).

"The Sociology of Language Learning and Teaching in a Creole Situation", *Sociological Abstracts: Supplement* 82, no. 1 (August 1978), published in the *Caribbean Journal of Education* 5, no. 3 (1978).

"A Creole English Continuum and the Theory of Grammar", in *Papers from the 1975 International Conference on Pidgin and Creole Languages*, in *Varieties of English around the World*, edited by R.R. Day, vol. 2 (Heidelberg: Julius Groos Verlag, 1980).

"English Language Teaching: Problems and Prospects in the West Indies", in *Education in the West Indies: Developments and Perspectives, 1948–1988: A Reader on the Occasion of the Fortieth Anniversary of the University of the West Indies* (Kingston: Institute of Social and Economic Research, University of the West Indies, 1996).

"Creolistics and Education", in *Anglistentag 1989 Wurzburg: Proceedings*, edited by Rudiger Ahrens (Tubinger: Max Niemeyer Verlag, 1990).

Abbreviations

Adj	adjective
Adv	adverb
Indef. Art.	indefinite article
JC	Jamaican Creole
N_{an}	noun animate
N_{inan}	noun inanimate
N_{hum}	noun human
N_f	noun feminine
N_m	noun masculine
NC	noun constituent/ cluster
NP	noun phrase
Pred. Adv.	predicative adverb
S	sentoid / sentence
SS	sentences
S_1/S_2	speaker 1/ speaker 2
SE	Standard English
SVO	subject/verb/object
TOP	topicalization
V	verb
VP	verb phrase

Introduction

The Linguistic Contribution of Dennis Craig to Language Learning and Teaching in the English-official Caribbean

JEANNETTE ALLSOPP

D ennis Roy Craig (1929–2004) was one of the most outstanding Caribbean linguists of the twentieth century, a noted creolist and also a seminal fig-ure in the field of language education in the English-official Caribbean. Apart from this, Craig was also a distinguished figure in educational leadership in the region. He was vice dean and head of the teaching section (1975–77 and 1982–82) in the School of Education on the Mona campus (Jamaica) of the University of the West Indies. He was also the university dean of the Faculty of Education of the three campuses of the University of the West Indies (1982–85), director of the National Centre for Educational Resource Development in the Ministry of Education, Guyana (1988–91) and, subsequently, the vice-chancellor of the University of Guyana (1991–95), filling all of these roles in his traditional calm and cool, though firm and decisive manner, and piercingly perceptive in his insightfulness when it came to assessing situations and making decisions.

However, it is with his contribution as a linguist, particularly to language education in the Commonwealth Caribbean with which this book is concerned, and to that end, eight of his most representative articles have been chosen for this volume. The intention here is to demonstrate Craig's deep commitment to, and understanding of the language situation in the English-official Caribbean and the breadth of his vision in relation to the spheres of language teaching and language learning in the English-based Creole-speaking societies of the Commonwealth Caribbean.

The fact is that although most of these articles were written between the 1970s and the 1990s, much of the material that they deal with and the problems and issues that were identifiable during those decades have hardly changed although we are now in the twenty-first century. This state of affairs bears testimony to Craig's amazing grasp of the nature of the factors involved in the teaching and learning of language in Creole-speaking communities. It is hoped that this book will prove useful not only to language teachers but also to creolists as well as to practitioners and researchers in the field of Caribbean language education.

The articles that have been chosen are the following: "Education and Creole English in the West Indies: Some Sociolinguistic Factors " (1971), "Bidialectal Education: Creole and Standard in the West Indies" (1976), "Reading and the Creole Speaker" (1978), "The Sociology of Language Learning and Teaching in a Creole Situation" (1978), "Creole and Standard: Partial Learning, Base Grammar and the Mesolect" (1978), "English Language Teaching: Problems and Prospects in the West Indies" (1988), "A Creole English Continuum and the Theory of Grammar" (1980) and finally "Creolistics and Education" (1990).

The articles follow a chronological order and begin at the point where Craig identifies and explains the factors that impact on the language situation in the officially English-speaking Caribbean. The articles "Education and Creole English in the West Indies", "Creole and Standard", "Bidialectal Education", "English Language Teaching", "Reading and the Creole Speaker" and "The Sociology of Language Learning and Teaching in a Creole Situation" all focus on issues highly pertinent to the language situation in the officially English-speaking Caribbean and the sociolinguistic factors which influence language use, language learning and language teaching.

Creole as the Majority Language of the English-official Caribbean

First of all, Craig points out that that English-based Creole is the everyday language of the majority in the territories of the English-official Caribbean and that the basic features of English-based Creoles are very similar, and second, that the social structure of the territories involved is also similar because of the imposition of colonization and plantation slavery that took place in the seventeenth and eighteenth centuries. Consequently, although most of the articles deal largely with speakers of Jamaican Creole (JC), the findings as reported by Craig in relation to the sociolinguistic features he identifies therein are relevant to the territories of the English-official Caribbean in general.

Interaction Area, Interlanguage, Mesolect

In addition, Craig points out that there is an "interaction area" between the Creole and the Standard, intermediate between the two extremes of the continuum as defined for Jamaica by Bailey and Cassidy, whereby a third level is produced by "mixing" and what he terms "mutation with mixing", the latter in particular reflecting the complex social relationships that underlie it. It is the same "interaction area" that is referred to in some of the other articles, such as "Creole and Standard", when he refers to that mid-level area as the "mesolect", and "interlanguage" and points out that the variety being discussed is neither the Creole nor the Standard. The importance of language use to social mobility is shown to be crucial as is the fact that the language situation in the officially English-speaking Caribbean is closely interwoven with its social and economic development. Craig also illustrates the socially important contrasts at the phonological level and the lack of understanding demonstrated by the educational authorities who are incapable of producing creative and informed language policies that would improve the level of performance by the students in Standard English, which is the desired goal of English-teaching in all the territories.

He goes on to discuss the consequences of language teaching to children to whom English is neither a native nor a foreign language, that the majority of these children are far more capable of recognizing Standard English than of producing it and added, to make the argument more current, that the explosion of the Internet, text messaging and other similar communications media only compound the problem. Craig then looks in greater detail at a sample of Creole-speaking children in Jamaica and Trinidad who were tested on their learning of structural patterns to measure their rate of acquisition of the Standard in relation to the attitudes to the language. There is also an attempt on his part to differentiate between genders, as he looked at the results of boys versus girls in the production of standard speech involving verb phrases. These results showed that boys tended to produce fewer standard verb patterns than girls, although initially, there was little difference, but he perceived that the attitudes of the boys towards producing correct standard speech was that it was somewhat "sissyish" to produce that kind of language, whereas the girls were more aware of the social prestige attached to correct speech.

Restricted versus Elaborated Code

Most of the articles cited look at the language situation and the syntactic structuring on the part of Creole-speaking children in the English-official Caribbean against the theory of restricted versus elaborated code as put forward by Basil Bernstein in his research into sociolinguistic factors that applied in the case of the language production of British children. Craig did his own experiments with Jamaican children and was able to conclude that there are three types of difference between restricted and elaborated codes, such as those between discrete morpho-syntactic systems, difference in use within the context of speech and differences in cognitive orientation. He recognized the fact that the dialectal differences in the English-official Caribbean would impact more on their production of language than they would in the case of English working-class children among whom there are no such sharply defined differences, so that the learning of linguistic conventions would help the latter group to produce language that is nearer to the elaborated code than the Caribbean Creole-speaking children. He felt that the cognitive purposes to which language is applied and which would include not only morpho-syntactic, but also semantic variables would create difficulties for the learning of the Standard on the part of Creole-speaking children. That fact had not really been taken into consideration previously, but at the time of his writing was now beginning to be recognized in the work of Katz and Fodor (1964), Chomsky (1965) and also by Rickford (1974), who pointed out that African American Vernacular English (AAVE) shows similarities with Caribbean English Creoles as they certainly had an impact on the development of AAVE, given the historical conditions prevailing at the time when that variety was being shaped.

Issues Arising in the Teaching of Standard English

Another of Craig's concerns in the articles is that although the presence of a language continuum between the Creole and the Standard in the English-official Caribbean leads to an educational situation that is virtually bidialectal, and his contention that such a situation needs more than merely teaching the standard dialect without interfering with the child's home dialect, educational authorities refuse to see the point and to produce language policies that would address the issue. In "Bidialectal Education" and "English Language Teaching" he refers to the persistence on the part of teachers in teaching English "by correction", which results from there being no educational use of Creole or Creole-influenced language in the education systems of the territories under discussion. An alternative to this "teaching by correction" is of course Velma Pollard's *From Jamaican Creole to Standard English* ([1988] 2003), which proposes a comparative approach between the two varieties in a creative way and suggests viable and valuable activities that can be used to make the comparative approach more meaningful to students.

Having broached this question, Craig points out via examples of two types of mesolectal speech, taken from Rickford, that it is relatively easy for Creole speakers to get to a mesolectal level, but they find it difficult to move beyond that, and he also shows why nonstandard speakers who are at a similar mesolectal level tend to remain there. Of course, this is because there is great similarity between the semantic and syntactic strategies performed by the learner in the Creole and in the mesolect, but then new strategies are required for the move from the mesolect to the Standard.

We might therefore assume that the structure of conceptual knowledge is the same for all human beings and also that language is a means of labelling concepts. Such assumptions lead to the conclusion that conceptual and linguistic knowledge of speakers in relation to any meaningful segment of language are related and have a general structure, as set out in diagram 8 in "Creole and Standard". The diagram suggests that concepts occurring in the mind might possibly be given one-on-one lexical and syntactic labels simultaneously, which would constitute the first level of language, so sentence output here would be at the simplest lexical and syntactic level. Thereafter would come transformational processes involving the movement, deletion and grouping of already theoretically existing labels and the relabelling (lexicalization) of the grouped meanings would lead successively to more and more complex levels of syntax from Level 2 to whatever level the individual could manage.

The crux of the argument just set out is that the Creole is both lexically and syntactically simpler than the standard because the Creole is output made at an earlier level than standard language is. Nevertheless, conceptually, cognitively or semantically, the two types of language stem from the same base before and at Level 1. This fact has not been understood by the proponents of theories of linguistic and cognitive deficit in regard to speakers of non-standard languages, pidgins or Creoles or lower social class speakers generally. Craig's proposition is that there is a base grammar of every language and that the base grammar is the same for all languages. After Level 1, all languages would increase in grammatical complexity as they develop but each language could also adopt its own grammatical and lexical alternatives peculiar to itself, which would account both for grammatical diversity and grammatical similarity between languages. This is an interesting theory that is primarily developmental and moves away from the "deficit" theories that were proposed during the time of Craig's writing.

He then continues to discuss a number of additional reasons for the differences between the Creole and the Standard, giving translations of examples of Creole speech to the Standard and accounts for the fact that because the procedures outlined are present in standard language, but not in Creole, Creole and mesolectal speakers who try to produce standard language tend to make the types of mistakes that arise from their inability to extend and hold grammatical relationships across sentence boundaries. Similar to this is the inability of the Creole speaker learning to read the Standard to make the connections between parts of the sentence or separate sentences indicated by various morpho-syntactic and semantic items in the reading material, dealt with in the next article.

"Reading and the Creole Speaker" illustrates clearly Craig's engagement as a Caribbean language educator. In this article he looks at the problems involved in the teaching of reading to the Creole speaker, and more specifically the Jamaican Creole (JC) speaker, who serves as the representative example of the whole.

The two main tasks involved in teaching reading are identified, the first one being the need to associate the lexical items of English-based Creole with similar Standard English items as well as the need to link the printed shapes with the meanings they represent, which would present significant difficulties to the Creole speaker whose knowledge of Standard English vocabulary would certainly be limited. The second task is the ability to vocalize written or printed meanings through English sounds, as opposed to word-forms and syntax. He gives examples of the English sounds which would have corresponding Creole sounds in relation to pronunciation, but as he stresses, the desire of the teacher of English in general would be for the Creole-speaking student to produce perfectly correct English sounds, a highly unrealistic expectation. Craig feels that a better purpose might be served if English pronunciation were taught separately and apart from the teaching of reading, which might produce some progress in the Creole speaker's reading.

Craig goes on to point out the problem which would arise out of the second task in terms of word-forms and syntax, because of the following: (a) the fact that English possesses many inflections and grammatical forms that are not found in the Creole, such as singular/plural nouns that would signal particular verb forms that might occur in the reading passage later on, (b) adverbs of time and aspect that would also indicate specific tenses whereas Creole only has a base verb, (c) the inflected English pronominal system that would indicate inter-relationships between themes and topics in the reading material, and of course (d) English sentence-forms that are totally absent in the Creole, such the use of the copula and the use of "there is/there are" to start a sentence, also totally absent in Creole, and finally (e) the topicalization found in Creole that is non-existent, and so expressed differently in English, but highly prevalent in Creole.

As usual, Craig suggests the possible use of strategies to overcome such problems, such as (a) the Creole speaker being taught to read in language familiar to his/her environment then helped to transfer those skills to reading in English which is deemed unacceptable for various reasons, (b) giving the Creole speaker material that is controlled so that only English word-forms and grammar already present in the Creole are used, and (c) that reading and the basic structures of English be taught concurrently so that the Creole speaker becomes familiar with the form of the language that he or she is learning to read. This would require that structural language practice be done simultaneously and closely integrated with the reading programme offered.

Another issue raised by Craig is the neglect and rediscovery of Creole, the first aspect being produced by the type of postcolonial societies being discussed, and the rediscovery stemming from about the 1940s onwards when Creoles actually began to be formally studied by a number of Caribbean and North American linguists, such as the work appearing in Hymes (1971), and studies pertaining to information needed by the educator in relevant situations, such as Carrington (1976, 1969), Allsopp (1965), Bailey (1971), Winford (1972), Christie (1969).

Craig also looks at the pragmatic aspect of language use and the difference between the groups as related to context, purpose and situation, as different speakers exist in different cultural environments so that the content and purposes of their individual discourse would be different. To teach the Standard dialect, a particular communication style has to be taught also, so that the teacher can take independent language strings, separate from the lower-class communication style, and guide the child through the transformations that would convert such strings into an opposite communication style. Without such learning, many non-standard speakers who succeed in mastering the basic morpho-syntax of the Standard will continue to operate at a relatively low receptive level, a fact that is only revealed when such speakers begin to experience the demands of higher education.

The conclusion he reached is that the total requirements of bidialectal education include a full utilization of the child's cultural environment, while developing in the child the knowledge, skills, attitudes and cultural attributes necessary for social mobility, so that it can be seen that the acquisition of Standard language requires more than the acquisition of phonology, morphology and syntax and this realization is important for second-dialect teaching.

In "English Language Teaching", Craig raises some of the same concerns that he had done previously and he laments the fact that native language teaching approaches are still so firmly entrenched and points to fact that despite the wide range of English language teaching materials that have been published, only a fraction of educators have considered the principles set out to be worthy of serious consideration in the teaching process. He attributes the lack of change in teaching methods and approaches to the nature of those in charge of the teacher-training process, who are largely English literature graduates and notes that there are still teacher-trainers who will proudly say that they have no use for the "boring 'drill methods'" of second language or second-dialect teaching.

Also teaching for habit-formation in English is not pursued and young teachers in training are continually frustrated in their efforts to bring new and creative teaching strategies to the English language classroom. However, the ever-mounting pressure for improved performance in Standard English will hopefully drive teachers to finding more explicit ways of teaching it.

The article "The Sociology of Language Learning and Teaching in a Creole Situation" treats similar preoccupations on the part of the writer with the characteristics of Creole-speech communities relevant to education, with Creole-Standard bilingualism, bound up with the socio-economic status of the individual but not likely to be acquired with any facility between social class extremes, because of the social attitudes to the Standard versus those to the Creole and the need for territories to have a national official language that is also internationally acceptable. Those speakers who achieve Creole-Standard bilingualism are likely to code-switch from one to the other in a single conversation, and the mixing that takes place between the two "languages" does not make for any form of language that has a population of speakers.

There is the warning that the interlanguage which results from the intermediate varieties found between the Creole and the Standard along the post-Creole continuum will continue to be used by those Creole speakers with a high motivation to achieve upward social mobility, but if the community develops clear function roles for a Creole language, as has happened in Haiti, then the tendency of Standard speakers to acquire the Creole might result. The nature of the language situation in Creole-Standard bilingual communities has clear implications for the formation of a relevant language policy, while the ignoring of the Creole in education which tends to be the norm, will still not make Creole-speaking children motivated to speak the Standard.

Again attitudes to language are relevant in relation to the motivational factor, as the Standard language may be perceived by boys as a language "for sissies". Furthermore, the fact that Creole learners of the Standard are learning a language that is neither native nor foreign, will have implications for teaching methodology, which has to take account of the fact that communication styles differ between Creole and Standard speakers, though the communication strategies of the lower-social class communication format can achieve the same cognitive results as the strategies that are characteristic of Standard language. Craig points out that the significance of these wider issues for the sociology of language learning and teaching is that they indicate the commonalities underlying the structure and the functioning of the human being, but also suggest that selective procedures are put into effect by social groupings in relation to intangible factors such as linguistic structure.

In the abstract to the penultimate article, Craig claimed that previous studies of continuum situations adopted grammatical formulations that are incapable of representing the linguistic knowledge of the speaker in such situations. He indicates that what is needed is a grammar that is capable of representing the invariant conceptual element that can underlie syntactic and lexical variation and that can show the relationships between syntactic and lexical forms. He offers some proposals towards such a grammar and discusses some implications in relation to variation studies and socially determined differences in the use of language.

The article deals with the need for the type of grammar that realistically reflects the Creole English continuum. The prevailing contemporary theories of the time as put forward by Labov who opted to use Chomskyan approaches, Bickerton who proposed polylectal grammars, albeit with a Chomskyan base component, and Fraser who suggested that polylectal grammars might be more explanatory if they are related to the general syntagtactics and phonotactics of language considered as a static system were not satisfactory to Craig. It is also suggested that a deeper look at variation might serve as the base for investigating what a language continuum has to say about the native speaker's linguistic knowledge and how this structure might be represented as grammar.

Craig goes on to deal with various aspects of grammar within the continuum such as the function of nouns in relation to JC rules re the stating of what someone wants to do as a profession, for example, the minimal SVO sentence in relation to the expression of active versus passive, the analysis of a simple sentence, the use of transitive and intransitive verbs, the various uses of the noun phrase, affirmative and negative sentences, lexical "passing" and how all of these elements contribute to the formulation of a grammar that correctly reflects language use within the framework of the Creole continuum. The article also shows that after the series of lexical "passes" illustrated, all the necessary lexis, apart from abstract nouns and nominalizations would have been generated. It is expected that further processes involving rearrangements of syntactic components of sentences would continue to apply to the grammar to produce all possible items of syntax and lexis. The preceding outline given should then be adequate to suggest the general form of the grammar that seems necessary if the phenomena of the mind illustrated in the Creole-English continuum are to be accounted for.

The final article, "Creolistics and Education" refers to the study of the combination of language policy, planning and education in Creole-language situations which were termed "applied creolistics" by John Reinecke. Craig points out that the systematization of the data resulting from Creole studies has made it possible for applied creolistics to be meaningful and to contribute to the development of pidgin/Creole influenced societies.

The remainder of the article deals with relevant characteristics of Creole-language situations which have been set out in some of the previous articles. For example, the fact that monolingual Creole speakers tend to be persons of low social status, so that as a consequence their Creole is not accepted: that there is a very strong relationship between language and culture, that the structural form of Creoles is similar and that there have been theories of monogenesis as subscribed to by Thompson, Taylor and Stewart among others. Reference is also made to a special theory called "Afrogenesis" put forward by Richard Allsopp, who claimed that the source of the structural similarity of Creole languages is not a previous pidgin, but West African languages themselves. Craig goes on to discuss further the structural similarities existing between Creoles and looks at the conditioning of children in Creole-language situations who are affected by social class factors, a question also dealt with previously. He also looks at education policies and their determinants in relation to primary education and at modes of teaching reading to Creole-speaking children . He also discusses the principles put forward by Carrington in relation to both the linguistic factors involved as well as the socio-economic factors and of course prevailing attitudes to language. In addition, teaching the Standard in decreolized situations is discussed as is the need for a distinctive methodology for such teaching and the conclusion arrived at is that in Creole or Creole-language influenced situations, education needs to make use of applied creolistics so as to specify those features of Creole situations which provide a psycholinguistic conditioning that need to be taken into account in all classroom activity of schools, even though it may not be taken into consideration in determining language policy at the national level. Despite the fact that the movements to promote the Creoles and recognize them as national languages in the 1970s has waned, creolistics is nevertheless necessary to ensure that the psycholinguistic background of the Creole speaker be taken into consideration, especially in relation to the formulation of language policy.

Although this is a small sample of the work of Dennis Craig, it is representative of his linguistic thought and his linguistic contribution to education. His investigation into the conditions existing in the English-official territories of the Caribbean and his study of all aspects of the language situation in these territories has certainly shed light on the need to develop the kind of educational practice that does not ignore the presence of the Creole as the native language of the majority of English-based Creole speakers, but takes full account of it. The proposals and suggestions put forward by Craig to combat the social and linguistic disadvantages faced by Creole-speaking members of society via education are highly commendable. However, unfortunately, many of the same conditions that he encountered in his research so many years ago still prevail, as does the lack of any progressive and meaningful language policy within most of the Creole-speaking territories of the English-official Caribbean, despite ongoing research.

References

Allsopp, S.R.R. 1965. "British Honduras : The Linguistic Dilemma". *Caribbean Quarterly* 11 (3–4).

Bailey, B. 1971 . "Jamaican Creole: Can Dialect Boundaries Be Defined?" In *Pidginization and Creolization of Language*, edited by D. Hymes. Cambridge: Cambridge University Press.

Carrington, L. 1969. "Deviations from Standard English in the speech of primary school children in St Lucia and Dominica". *IRAL* 8 (3).

———. 1976. "Determining Language Education Policy in Caribbean Sociolinguistic Complexes". *International Journal of the Sociology of Language* 8.

Chomsky, N. 1965. *Aspects of the Theory of Syntax*. Cambridge, MA: MIT Press.

Christie, P. 1969. "A Sociolinguistic Study of some Dominican Creole Speakers". PhD diss., University of York.

Hymes, D., ed. 1971. *Pidginization and Creolization of Language*. Cambridge: Cambridge University Press.

Katz, J.J., and J.A. Fodor, eds. 1964. *The Structure of Language*. Englewood Cliffs, NJ: Prentice-Hall.

Pollard, V. [1988] 2003. *From Jamaican Creole to Standard English: A Handbook for Teachers*. Kingston: University of the West Indies Press.

Rickford, J. 1974. "The Insights of the Mesolect". In *Pidgins and Creoles: Current Trends and Prospects*, edited by D. DeCamp and I. Hancock. Washington, DC: Georgetown University Press.

Winford, D. 1972. "A Sociolinguistic Description of Two Communities in Trinidad". PhD thesis, University of York.

1 | Education and Creole English in the West Indies

Some Sociolinguistic Factors

The newly emerging nations of the former British West Indian[1] colonies now known as the English-official Caribbean – Guyana, Trinidad, Barbados, Jamaica, the rest of the English-speaking Windward and Leeward Islands, and Belize (British Honduras) – face social and educational problems directly attributable to the fact that forms of English Creole speech are the everyday language of the majority of their populations. Of such speech, that of Jamaica is best known (cf. Le Page and DeCamp (1960), Cassidy (1961), Bailey (1962, 1966), and Cassidy and Le Page (1967)). The differences between Jamaican Creole and other varieties of English Creole in these nations are minor, and Bailey's summary of the principal differences between Jamaican Creole and English Syntax (Bailey 1966:146) can stand as a summary of known differences between English and most English-based Caribbean Creoles. In addition to the basic similarity of speech there is corresponding similarity in social structure. The social traditions and institutions have evolved from common origins in seventeenth- and eighteenth-century British colonial plantation systems based on the enslavement of Africans, and at present all the territories remain small societies with large, poor African working classes, small middle-classes mainly in bureaucratic occupations, seriously underdeveloped economies, and social status requirements, including language patterned on the British model. These similarities between individual territories lend some justification to the ensuing attempt to consider the Caribbean English Creole language situation as a whole with regard to some of the sociolinguistic phenomena it has produced.

The Interaction Area between Creole and Standard

In recognizing the existence of the Creoles, it has been necessary to recognize also what has been referred to as the 'continuum' between Creole and Caribbean Standard English. This fact needs no treatment here, having been adequately dealt with in the works cited above, and in Bailey (1964) and the papers by Bailey and DeCamp in this volume [*Pidginization and Creolization of Language*, edited by Dell Hymes]. A theoretical model for Jamaica (Craig 1966), one which seems relevant also to the other territories, conceives the language situation as a dynamic interrelationship of forms of speech, such as shown in (1a, 1b).

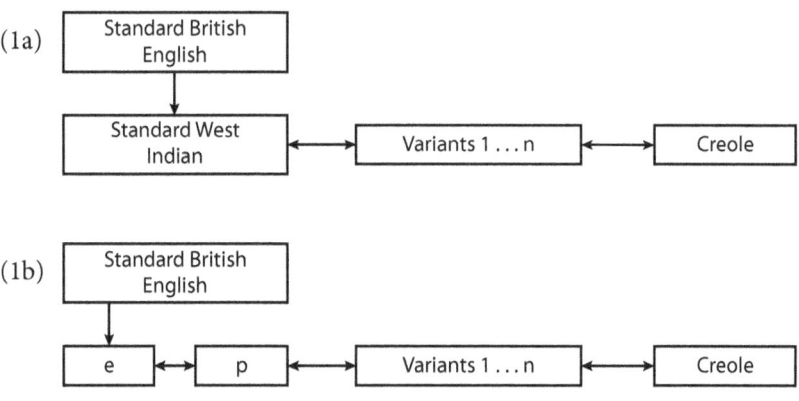

In the second diagram Standard Caribbean English speech, as accepted in formal social situations, is analysed into two components; p represents the ways in which such speech differs from Standard British English. There is a one-way channel of influence from SBE to SCE and to p, but p is linked to the rest of the system by two-way channels. The rest of the system consists of a range of linguistic variation (variants 1, 2, 3, . . .n), which together with p, represents an *area of interaction* between the community's social standard and Creole speech. Influence flows both ways.

This area of interaction is intermediate between the extremes of the continuum defined for Jamaica by Bailey and DeCamp. I refer to it as 'interaction' because its existence has been, and continues to be, dependent on the cross-influences from the two extremes.

DeCamp (1968) points out that 'given two samples of Jamaican speech which differ substantially from one another, it is usually possible to find a third intermediate level in an additional sample'. In thinking of the continuum as 'interaction', however, it becomes possible to formulate a social corollary:

(2)   A speaker aiming to produce a significantly less familiar, but socially required system of speech usually produces a system intermediate between his most familiar one and the one aimed at.

The importance of this formulation is that it emphasizes individual behaviour and the individual acts of speech that go to make up a continuum; the origin of the continuum in varying social requirements for language; and that what otherwise might have been a stratification of a few discrete kinds of speech is indeed made into a continuum by the cumulative results of mutual *interference* or 'interaction' between linguistic systems. In brief, the end of the processes outlined in (1) and (2) is a continuum, one compatible with the analyses of Bailey and Decamp, but one whose existence and sociolinguistic implications cannot be adequately accounted for except in terms of interaction and mutual interference. (A linguistic 'system' here denotes any given set of interrelationships among linguistic forms, irrespective of the extent of overlapping in features with other such sets.)

There seem to be two main ways in which interaction between linguistic systems creates a continuum. The first is well illustrated in DeCamp's Table 1, and may be called 'simple mixing'. In simple mixing, different speakers use different combinations of the contrasts provided by two relatively widely separated systems. DeCamp's examples show six contrasts and seven combinations of these, and demonstrate that the combinations are rule-governed.

The second mode of interaction also involves mixing, but before mixing occurs, the original contrasts seem to be mutated in various ways, sometimes through interference of one system with the other. I refer to this second type as 'mutation with mixing'. Examples can be seen in the following:

(3)   **Some socially significant contrasts**

Standard extreme	Intermediate	Creole extreme
'didn't'	/din/, /in/, no/, /na/	/no ben/, /na bin/
'it's' /iz/	/a/	
'want to go'	/waan(t) guo/	/waan fi (fo) guo/ gʌ
'bay' [bei]	/beə/	/bɪə/˚
'potato' [puteitou]	/puteto:/,/putetə/	/pəteta/, /pitieta/

˚See DeCamp, Table 2.

Mutated items, such as those in the intermediate column of (3), would be subject to the rules of social selection mentioned by DeCamp. A speaker who uses /in/ for 'didn't', for example, would not have the same combined substitutions (of the type of DeCamp's Table 1) as a speaker who uses /na/ or /no/. The combined processes of mutating and mixing produce the extreme complexity of the so-called continuum and express the social relationships that underlie it.

The complexity would be even more apparent if segments of discourse, rather than isolated lexical items, were contrasted. Thus, two contrasting, and referentially equivalent statements, from the extremes, such as:

(4)   'He's her uncle'/shi a fi(fo) kaaal im (i) oŋkl/

would be represented by a lengthy range of socially significant variants, including a pronunciation of 'She is to call him uncle' that many speakers would unhesitatingly accept as belonging to Caribbean Standard English.

Language and Social Mobility

The situation outlined above reflects a striving on the part of a former Creole-speaking population toward a model provided by Standard British English and the social mobility it confers, a striving that has created the specific forms of Caribbean Standard English to be found in the different territories. Bailey's comment (1966:106) about Jamaica is as true for the entire English-speaking Caribbean today as it has undoubtedly always been:

> It is possible to move from one social class to another by changing one's linguistic norm. This is of course due to another factor, the correlation between a good

education and acceptable English, which makes it possible to assume that ability to manipulate JSE Jamaican (Standard English) is indicative of a good education, in addition of course, to birth in a higher caste or class.

In this striving for social status through English, the axiom stated in (2) above becomes reality, and speakers create the interaction area. Younger people encounter this upward social striving at an early age. It is a long-standing practice in many places for children who do not 'talk proper', or who 'talk bad', to be scolded into producing a 'better' kind of speech. Many parents, who may be able to shift somewhat into the interaction area, but whose own repertoire is normally Creole, do this. I have had experience of this in Guyana and have witnessed such scolding in Jamaica, St Vincent, Grenada, and Trinidad. The result is that by early school age some children have become able to shift their speech into the interaction area, even though their home is mostly Creole-speaking. The speech of most other children is brought into this area by formal schooling and the influence of the mass media. At present it would seem that the spontaneous as well as careful speech of a majority of school-age children lies entirely within the interaction area. That is, it is neither Creole nor standard Caribbean, nor yet again does it represent a discrete, stable speech norm of its own. It is, in other words, an interlanguage.

The examples in (5) below are typical of the responses teachers have been observed to obtain when trying to get children to 'correct' spontaneous utterances. Each of the sets 5(i) to 5(viii) comes from a different child, usually in a different place (since these items are only chance records made by the writer in visits to schools in Jamaica, Trinidad and Guyana). The children range in age from 7 to 12 years.

(5) **Spontaneous utterance and attempts of the same child at 'careful' standard-language replacement**   **Creole and Standard versions not heard**

   (i) /a mi buk dat/   /a fi mi buk dat/
      /iz mi buk/   *'It's my book.'*
      /iz mai buk/
  (ii) /a bin tu di stuor/   /mi bin a stuor/
      /ai did guo tu di stuor/   *'I went to the store.'*
 (iii) /we i de/   /a we i de/
      /wier hi iz/   *'Where is he?'*

(iv) /shi brokop di pliet/	(This seems already to be the Creole form)
/shi briek di pliet/	*'She's broken the plate.'*
/a waan letout/	/mi waan (fu) letout/
(v) /ai waant tu letout/	*'I want to be let out' i.e. . . . to be allowed to go outside*
(vi) /a in get non/	*/mi na bin get non/*
/ai didn get non/	*'I didn't get any.'*
(vii) /iz kot yu waan kot it/	/a kot yu waan (fu) kot i/
(viii) /yu waan kot it/	*'Do you want to cut it?'*
/yu in si yu a mash mi fut/	/yu na bin, si se yu a mash mi fut/
/yu sii yu mash mai fut/	*'Don't you see you are mashing (stepping on) my foot?'*

Note that the attempt to switch from one level of speech to another is sometimes accompanied, as is to be expected, by a reduction in expressiveness, as in (iv), (vii) and (viii). Apart from this, however, the kind of ability displayed by most children as in (5) results on the whole in a surprising paradox. For a vast majority of young people, this ability fails to develop any further, so that they leave school and attain adulthood without being able to shift out of the interaction area into the highly-prized standard-language extreme of the continuum. The apparent facility with which these young speakers operate within the interaction area seems incompatible with the apparently difficult barrier that they find between this facility and the highly-prized goal of standard language. The likely reason for this and the important educational implications that arise will be shown in the next section.

The early age at which children learn to switch linguistic forms in the presence of elders, teachers and strangers in general, given the evidently vital social significance of language in the English-speaking Caribbean, seems to indicate that the stages of 'social perception' and 'stylistic variation' *begin much earlier and at the same time are probably more prolonged for West Indian children* than for the New York children described by Labov (1964:91). [Eds: Since this article was written Labov's methods of correlating linguistic and social variables have been used in sociolinguistic research in Caribbean language by linguists such as John Rickford.]

Academic interest in the interaction between Creole and standard language has an importance which goes beyond the mere perfecting of sociolinguistic theory, important as the latter is. Such interest in the West Indies is essential to the provision of guidelines for social action, specifically educational action in respect of language. The language situation in the English-official Caribbean is intimately bound up with economic and social development. Large sectors of the non-standard speaking population (estimated at about 80% of the total population) have to be educated, and rapidly so, for functioning in a modern economy; and Standard English, by way of text-books, instructors, examinations etc., is the medium through which this is being attempted. The societies in all territories are, in a way, trapped within their Standard English traditions; widespread inability to use the standard language is resulting in increasing wastage in expanding educational systems, wastage which poor economies cannot afford. Official government statements in all the territories, apart from putting increasing emphasis on the social-mobility value of English and condemning school examination results (which often give a failure rate at all levels between 60 and 85% in English in most territories) show very little insight into the real nature of the problem. [Eds: Consequently, no long-term remedies are being sought by the institutionalized education authorities in the English-official Caribbean. Rather, the problem is now compounded by the advent of the Internet and its by products of text messaging, etc.]

Consequences for Language Teaching

The factors so far outlined place the child in the English-official Caribbean in the kind of language-learning situation discussed by Stewart (1964) in which *English is neither a native language nor a foreign language.* It has been shown elsewhere (Craig 1966, 1967) that this unique language-learning situation is directly related to the interaction area discussed above and that, because of this, the language, Standard English, to be learned may be theoretically analysed into four strata:

(6)   Class A: Patterns actively known. That is, Creole or other non-standard speakers know how to use these spontaneously in their own informal speech.
Class B: Patterns used only under stress. These may have been learned, without becoming firmly habitual, through school teaching, through short contacts with Standard English speakers through intermittent exposure to mass media, etc.
Class C: Patterns known passively. That is, Creole or other non-standard speakers would understand these owing to context, if used by other speakers, but non-standard speakers would not themselves be able to produce

them, except as mutations within the interaction area or 'errors' relative to Standard English.

Class D: Patterns not known.

The evidence for this stratification in the English-language repertoire of Caribbean children comes from studies of the abilities of the speakers under several conditions:

(7)   (i)   Talking spontaneously with friends. (Samples of over 300 Jamaican children, and smaller numbers of children in Grenada and St Lucia recorded, in small peer-groups.)
   (ii) Talking in social situations requiring formal or 'careful' speech. Transcriptions of children talking on given topics to an interviewer in classroom situations in Jamaica, Trinidad, Guyana and some of the smaller territories. (In addition, corroborative evidence is supplied by samples of written composition of older children and young adults.)
   (iii) Comprehending standard speech. (Evidence from the results of classroom exercises in oral and reading comprehension and reported classroom observations of practising as well as trainee teachers.)

From 7(i) and 7(ii) it is possible to ascertain the range of children's speech within the interaction area and to divide this range into two sets of features corresponding to Classes A and B of illustration (6). Class (A) features (actively known) are those common to both 7(i) and 7(ii). Class B features are those which appear only under condition 7(ii). Standard English features appearing as mutations under condition 7(ii) would belong to Class C, but these as well as other features belonging to Classes C and D would be further revealed under condition 7(iii). In practice, especially when older learners are involved, it is not always possible to make a clear separation of Class C (passively known) from Class D (unknown) features, since some linguistic contexts are so helpful to speakers that the presence of an unknown feature has little or no effect on comprehension, except in very well controlled tests of a kind which it has not been possible to conduct up to now in the English-official Caribbean. It is sometimes convenient therefore to treat the two classes as one (Class C/D) in teaching methods, while acknowledging the theoretical difference between them. (See Appendix for illustration of stratification.)

The special implication of the stratification of the Standard English being learned is that *the learner is able all the time to recognize Standard English far out of proportion to his ability to produce it*. This happens chiefly because of Class C features which are either inherently redundant, or, as pointed out before, may be rendered so by the context, or are recognizable because of resemblance to mutations actually possessed by the speaker. These features, when combined with Classes A and B, create within the learner the illusion that the target Standard English is known already. This is reminiscent of the well-known distinction between the production and recognition levels of a learner's control of language (cf. Fries 1963) but the implications are not identical. Under normal circumstances a foreign learner's production and recognition repertoires of English are both initially non-existent. When acquired, they do not form a part of his native language repertoire; they remain separate and distinct. In the case of the Creole or other non-standard speaker, however, a basis for both already exists when he comes to learn Standard English, and they become, within the speaker, *the area of interaction* between his familiar speech and Standard English.

It was mentioned earlier that the apparently difficult speech barrier that some learners find between the interaction area and the Standard-English extreme of the continuum seems inconsistent with the ability of most speakers to use language from the interaction area. This situation is explainable in terms of the nature of the passively known (Class C) features relative to the rest of the stratification. The learning of Standard English can become arrested at a point where the quantity of unknown features (Class D) has become possible relative to formal social requirements, but at the same time the quantity of features known passively (Class C) has remained relatively large and significant. The speaker in this situation would possess an adequate 'recognition' of Standard English and a consequently strong sense of knowing the language. These dispositions would reduce both his motivation to modify his language as well as his ability to perceive contrasts between what language he actually produces and what he aims to produce. Only the social consequences of his Standard English efforts would be apparent to him. That this is the frustrating position in which many non-Standard- speaking learners find themselves seems abundantly clear from the examinations and other reports on English-language proficiency that appear in the English-official Caribbean year after year.

Owing directly to the high level of recognition mentioned above and to the fact that the *context* of speech, as a variable element, can always act to convert an unknown feature of Standard English into a passively known feature, the learner reacts in the following ways to normal *foreign language* teaching procedures:

(8) (i) The learner often fails to perceive new target elements in the teaching situation.

(ii) The reinforcement of learning which derives from the learner's satisfaction at mastering a new element, and knowing he has mastered it, is minimal.

(iii) Because of the ease of shifting from Standard English to Creole or other non-standard speech and vice-versa, the learner resists any attempt to restrict his use of Standard English within the Standard English patterns known to him in the teaching situation.

At the same time, *native language* methods, because they assume that the learner already knows the language being taught, fail to give him an active command over language patterns of Classes C and D. The English-official Caribbean territories have been committed to such methods in schools by history and social tradition, and abundant evidence of the results is to be perceived not only in linguistic but in social terms, in the complaints about school-leavers' proficiency and the general social anxiety referred to earlier.

English-teaching methods appropriate for the kind of language situation here discussed have been outlined in greater detail in sources cited already. The salient points about such methods are as follows:

(9)   (i) Foreign-language teaching techniques of grading and pattern drill can be used successfully mostly for unknown and only to a lesser extent for passively known patterns.

(ii) Since the learner's native speech and Standard English co-exist in the same everyday environment and since the aim of English-teaching, unlike that in a true foreign-language situation, is to replace the child's original language in the expectation that the child would switch to Standard English in most social situations, grading and pattern practice need to be integrated, more closely than in a normal foreign-language situation, with the learners' normal everyday requirements for language. This means that grading has to be strongly guided by the maturity, interests and experiences of specific learners, and contextual orientation on the whole plays a bigger role than it does in normal foreign-language teaching.

(iii) Because of (ii) and high recognition, pattern drills are less likely to yield the desired results of relatively spontaneous production of SE, since the latter variety is not a true foreign or second language, but a second dialect. The major methods of teaching require a more situational and communicative approach whereby chunks of language are learned in context and their use is also practised in context.

Pedagogical approaches such as the Oral Approach and Situational Language Teaching, the Natural Approach, and the Communicative Approach need to be applied to suit the language teaching/learning situation outlined above.

(iv) For effective use of situational and communicative methods, the patterns of Standard English must be grouped in such a way that a teaching-set would consist of an unknown or passively known element as target, together with such Class A or B elements as are necessary to create a simulated language 'situation'.

Such methods, when used with young, extreme or intermediate Creole-speakers, produce results which seem to support the theoretical position here discussed as to the interaction area between Creole and Standard English and the stratification of the learner's English repertoire that arises out of this. An illustration follows.

Language Acquisition and Attitudes

The learning of English by children possessing Creole or other non-standard speech appears to proceed not in clearly definable steps, but as a gradual process of linguistic change through the 'interaction area' earlier described. The process was studied with regard to five groups:

(10) E_1, E_2, E_3, E_4 = Four groups of rural Creole-speaking children who entered school for the first time at age 6 ½–7.

$E_{10}, E_{20}, E_{30}, E_{40}$ = The same groups of children after 6 months of learning English

C_1, C_{10} = A control group of children at the beginning (approximately) and end respectively of the experimental period.

The children's learning was measured at regular intervals by language production tests which required each child to talk freely about a given picture-card. The E groups were taught by the procedures stated in (9). The control group was taught by traditional native-language methods, but possessed an advantage over the experimental-groups in that it had previously had 2–3 years of infant education and had been involved in special native-language infant school projects. It was felt necessary to give the control group this advantage over the experimental groups in order to counterbalance a possible 'Hawthorne' effect in the experimental children. The criteria measured by the tests were a few which experience has shown to differentiate Creole and Standard-speaking children. These were:

(11)   (i)   The average proportion of clauses containing non-standard verb-phrases or non-standard relationships between nominative and verb.
       (ii) The average proportion of 'and'- linked clauses.
       (iii) The average number of words per clause.
       (iv) The quantity of intentionally formal speech (i.e. total number of words spoken) on a given occasion.

Criteria Measured in the Tests

Criteria	(i)	purely syntactic characteristics
	(ii)	a stylistic characteristic related to the fact that the Creole makes extensive use of /an/, 'and' in places of other types of linkage or terminal junctures within connected discourse
	(iii)	stylistic characteristic consisting of the use of many short coordinated clauses instead of longer, differently structured characteristics.
	(iv)	quantity of intentionally formal speech production

In relation to the criteria measured in the tests, Bernstein's claim of the use of a restricted code by lower-class children (1961) would need to be examined since there is some evidence that middle-class Jamaican children rate higher on (iii) and (iv) but lower on (ii) than lower-class children. Little or no change occurred in the control group, while the experimental groups changed significantly (see Appendix). For the experimental children, the attempt to learn English resulted in a gradual increase of their ability to move towards the standard-language extreme within the area of variation already described and *not in a restriction of their discourse (in formal social situations)* to *the purely standard forms they had learned*; this is shown by reduction without elimination of the Creole features with respect to criterion (i) especially. *The incipient English* repertoire *of the individual is evidenced as variation arising from a Creole/Standard English interaction.* In terms of the stratification illustrated in (6), this progress of learning may be envisaged as a progressive movement from any given stratum of the target repertoire to the one next above it.

This movement within the area of variation was accompanied by a normal growth in fluency and verbal planning ability as indicated by the increases shown with respect to criteria (iii) and (iv).

The children studied in (10) are Jamaican, but the situation they illustrate seems representative of the rest of the English-standard Caribbean as well, even though it is sometimes felt, especially in the absence of intensive linguistic study, that in the rest of the English-official Caribbean the Creole end of the 'continuum' is not as far removed from the English end as it is in Jamaica. However this may be, there is some evidence that the reduction of Creole characteristics just described is unusual for similar children in some other territories and that this is due to the specially controlled teaching methods (based on the stratification shown in (6) used with the Jamaican children. Comparable Trinidadian children from six schools in or around Port of Spain were tested and matched with the pooled Jamaican samples $E_{10} + E_{20} + E_{30} + E_{40} +$, of (10). The following is the result of the comparison:

(12)

	Jamaican special-tuition samples	Trinidad normal samples	Standard error	Level of signifi- cance
(i) Total number of words spoken (11, iv)	72.48	69.47	10.55	Not
(ii) Mean number of words per clause (11, iii)	4.94	4.66	0.50	Not
(ii) Proportion of non-standard verb phrases (11, i)	0.175	0.372	0.054	0.01

This shows that the proportion of non-standard verb-phrases in the Trinidadian children without special tuition, is significantly more than the proportion in the Jamaican children after tuition, even though the former were attending school a year earlier. Children in the English speaking Caribbean on the whole are unlikely to react very much differently from the children studied so far. This seems to support the conclusions earlier reached about the nature of the interaction area between English and Creole and its significance in the total language situation.

The examples come from young school children mainly because, in relation to the specific phenomena we refer to here, there is a paucity of data evidence from adult language. Given the accelerating economic development of the region and the relatively rapid social changes being brought about, however, the language of school children and young adults will most strongly be subject to the stresses which motivate linguistic change. This in itself is ample justification for more intensive and less superficial studies of young people's language than those producing the evidence discussed above.

Young people's motivation for linguistic change is related to their attitude to the language to be learned. It is likely that attitudes towards Standard English, though not necessarily clearly overt, will be strong and deep-seated. This matter has hardly been studied but there is some evidence that children as young as those studied may have the beginnings of definable attitudes toward standard speech. In one or two instances boys, when not aware of being observed by teachers, etc., amused themselves by somewhat exaggerated mimicry of girlish voices conveying bits of standard speech. The point of the mimicry seemed to be that *femininity or lack of toughness was to be associated with standard speech.* In the groups studied (10), girls' speech changed more extensively towards the prestige norms than boys did, although both changed. Thus when the groups E_{10}, E_{20}, E_{30}, E_{40} were pooled and analysed into boys and girls, the results were as follows:

(13)

Proportions of non-standard verb-phrases	Standard error	Significance of difference
Boys	0.29	0.075
Girls	0.065	0.01

The proportion of non-standard verb-patterns differed significantly between boys and girls. The girls showed the smaller proportion although initially there were no significant differences between boys and girls or between these children and control groups (Craig, 1967b). The preceding result could be due to differential rates of learning between boys and girls, as are sometimes evidenced in educational studies, but even so differential learning usually results from differences in underlying motivations. Attitudes and motivations of Creole speakers learning Standard English need much further investigation.

Relevance of the Theory of Restricted and Elaborated Codes

The presumed origins of Creole and the conditions perpetuating it in the English-official Caribbean are such as should have resulted in a syntactic structuring of Creole along the lines of a restricted code in the sense of Bernstein (1961, 1964, 1965, 1966). The kind of shared referential situations postulated by Bernstein as giving rise to restricted codes seem to correspond closely with what must have applied in the original contact situations producing the pidgin language which finally became Creole English. The working-class urban and rural conditions providing the social environment of Creole speech today likewise correspond with the postulated social contexts of restricted codes. When furthermore the syntactic structure of Caribbean English Creole speech is compared with that of Standard English it becomes evident that the main differences between the two correspond with some of the main predicted structural differences between restricted and elaborated codes. Some illustration of this correspondence is set out in (14).

(14)

Main peculiarities of English Creole syntax	*Predicted tendencies of speakers (in terms of a restricted code)*
(i) (a) No subject-verb concord (b) No case in pronouns (c) No sex in pronouns (Jamaica).	Considered together with (iii) below, clauses or sentences would need to be shorter rather than longer, simple preferably, have a referential domain known to speaker and listener so that subject-predicate relationships may be easily perceptible.
(ii) No passive form of the verb.	'A syntactic form stressing the active voice.' (Bernstein 1961)
(iii) No marking to indicate tense in the verb except by the use of a particle specifying 'past' and sometimes one specifying 'continuous'.	Reinforcement of predicated tendencies as for (i) with the burden of tense relationships being taken over by context.
(iv) (a) Predication of adjectives /Jan sik/= John (is) (was) (etc.) sick. (b) Associative plurals /Mieri-dem/ = Mary and her friends. /Di piipl dem/= all the people.	Modification of English in the direction of implicit rather than explicit meaning.

(v) (a) Reduplication.   Use of repetition resulting in a
        /wan-wan/ = a few here and   reduction in the range of required
        there.   lexis. Reinforcement of the ten-
        /taak-taak/ = talk all the time   dency in (iv).
        /huoli-huoli/ = full of holes.
    (b) Some uses of the 'inverted'
        sentence.
        /a ded im ded/ = he's really
        dead.

There can be little doubt that, as illustrated in (14) the production of Creole English would, in comparison with SE display fewer normal devices with which to
organize and treat subject-matter, but need not necessarily be viewed, as stated
by Bernstein, as a restricted code, but rather a higher and mere concise code.
However, there is a related aspect of the question to be considered, and that is,
the progressive increase in the available formal devices of the kind mentioned
above, evident in the repertoire of the Creole speaker as he/ she moves along the
continuum towards the acquisition of SE. In learning Standard English, a Creole
speaker or a speaker within the interaction area would experience this increase.
That the latter might indeed be so has already been evidenced incidentally; three
of the variables (12(ii) 'and'-linked clauses; 12(iii) length of clauses; 12(iv) quantity of speech) usually studied in the Bernstein type of investigations (cf. Bernstein
1962 (a and b), Lawton 1963 and 1964 and Robinson 1965) were noted to change
from restricted to elaborated-code proportions as the learning of Standard English progressed. Further, the children studied in the group E_4/E_{40} of (10) possessed
relatively less of 12(ii) and relatively more of 12(iii) and (iv) than the other children both at the beginning and end of the experimental period. The children of
E_4/E_{40} came predominately from relatively well-provided homes in an area where
most parents, even though of working-class occupations, were well-paid employ-
ees of a large bauxite company. Thus the group in E_4/E_{40} of (10) would possess a
background of middle-class influences not present in the other groups and this by
the Bernstein theory might account for the advantage it displays in the variables
stated. It would thus seem that some of the variables postulated as differentiating between social-class codal systems also differentiate Creole from Standard
English, and decrease or increase progressively over the range of the continuum,
viewed either for the language community taken as a whole or for the individual
passing from one point of the continuum to another through learning.

The preceding conclusions however, if valid, imply a contradiction in terms
since codal differences, of the kind postulated in the Bernstein theory, should

not be merely functions of different syntactic systems and be variable in the way they appear to be in the Creole/Standard English continuum. It is true that the individual syntactic and stylistic variables in (14) and (10) are only a very few of those considered in codal experiments so far, but as types they seem related to a large proportion of the variables postulated as differentiating codal systems (if we exclude for the moment certain lexical variables which appear different in nature, as will be indicated below). Thus, the assumed differences between restricted and elaborated codes may be analysed into three main types:

(15)   (i)   differences between discrete morpho-syntactic systems.
        (ii) differences in the use made of the context of speech.
        (iii) differences in cognitive orientation.

These three kinds of difference interact and influence each other, but they are quite distinct, and failure to distinguish between them seems to be a difficulty in the theory of restricted and elaborated codes.

Differences between discrete morpho-syntactic systems (15(i)) are evident to some extent in the Creole/Standard English continuum, but not in the type of situations so far assumed in Bernstein's theory. It seems doubtful, however, that such differences can be ruled out in considering social class differences in language, certainly at this stage of our knowledge. Differences in use made of the context of speech have to do with the contrast between situations in which meaning must be explicitly elaborated and situations in which shared under-standing allows or requires it to be left implicit. Most of the differences between restricted and elaborated codes belong to these two categories, or to the second alone. As shown earlier, the same differences are found between points in the Creole language continuum and Standard English.

What is important about these two sets of differences is that they can be reduced and no doubt eliminated by the learning of linguistic conventions. All that these two sets of differences represent is an adjustment in the use of morpho-syntactic and lexical elements to correspond with adjustments in the use of speech-context. In a situation such as that assumed in Bernstein's theory where there are no dialectal differences, the learning of these adjustments con-sists of learning to make a social adaption. In situation such as that assumed in Bernstein's theory, where there are no sharply defined dialectal differences, as in the Caribbean English language situation, the learning of these adjustments con-sists of learning to make a social adaption. This would account for the indications in the work of Lawton (1963, 1964) and Robinson (1963), that working-class English children probably have an elaborated code available for selected use and that working-class children who were Robinson's subjects, evinced more signs of restricted coding in 'informal' uses of language than middle class children did in the same, but that differences between the two classes of children were inconclusive when the 'formal' use of language was considered. Differences of the last sort seem likely because the working class children in the last instance had probably learned the necessary situational adaptions for formal-language usage, but at the same time, being more habituated than middle-class children in using the context of speech for conveying meaning, their informal use of language betrayed this habituation.

The third kind of codal difference, cognitive orientations, is the most fundamental, if it exists. These are differences which may be expected to arise because members of different socio-cultural identifications may be differently habituated in the kinds of situations demanding language, the kind if life-experiences that language treats as content, and the ways in which such experiences are apprehended and cognitively mediated through language. The prime importance of the Bernstein theory is that it relates this kind of human disposition to behavioural norms of social class. It is not often realized, however, that in this respect the theory is an intra-cultural version of the Whorfian hypothesis, corresponding to one of the two types of linguistic relativity discussed in Hymes (1966).The theory is of this kind because it seeks to make inferences from language, which is directly evidenced, to cognitive processes which are not, and the relationship between the two is a part of a cyclical process such as is diagrammed in (16).

It is precisely the linguistic-relativity aspect that makes it necessary for differences to be analysed as in (15). The assumed social-class codes approximate in form to the Creole/Standard-English continuum, but there one can postulate a range of discrete morpho-syntactic systems, each of which make as lesser or greater use of the context of speech. In such systems, a particular meaning or type of meaning that is mediated in one way in one system may be mediated in another way, but with a minimum of morpho-syntactic variation, in another system.

(16)

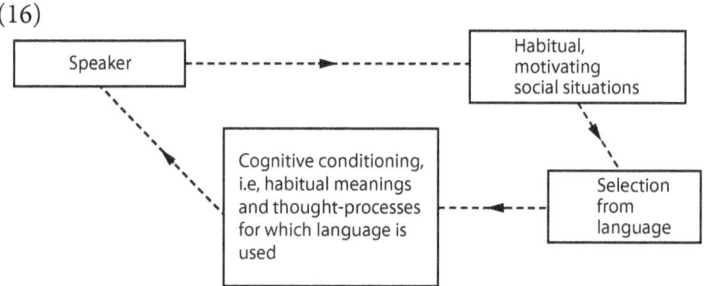

In such an assumed range of systems, it would be possible for different systems to give different functional loads to identical morpho-syntactic devices, or to eliminate or maintain different proportions of the natural redundancy of language; and these variations can occur without the possibility of doubt that the speakers involved are exercising equivalent linguistic capabilities, merely with different proportions of the two elements involved in the combination: 'morpho-syntax+context'.

If our theory then makes inferences about the cognitive orientation of speakers, there must be observable criteria other than the two already mentioned. There must be independent evidence that differences in cognitive orientation are involved. I refer to this third set of necessary criteria as *semantic* criteria, because it seems that this kind of concern can only be answered by relating selections of language to the sum of meanings that the speaker aims to convey, or is in the habit of conveying or is at all capable of conveying.

In the codal studies cited already, the concern to study certain lexical variables shows that the relevance of semantic considerations has been felt. The question at issue in testing the theory of restricted and elaborated coding was never, it seems to me, the form of the language used, nor exclusively whether one form of code used the context of speech to a greater extent than the other, but rather *the cognitive purposes to which language is applied*. Yet the methods of such study up to now, while permitting some attention to semantic variables, seem to attempt the measurement of cognitive purposes mainly in terms of the presence or absence of lexical and morpho-syntactic elements without being able to make any measurement of the possible semantic *equivalence* of different combinations of lexis, morpho-syntax and the use of context.

When the samples of speech tested for codal differences are, on the one hand, an extreme or intermediate form of Creole and, on the other, Standard English, and are thus close enough to be compared as social-class codes, though differing sufficiently to justify a search for semantic equivalences of the kind mentioned, then the need for more penetrating methods of language analysis becomes evident. Until recently, methods of studying semantic relationships held little promise of providing efficient tools for the study of codal systems. Over the past few years, however, the work of Katz and Fodor (1964) and Chomsky (1965) in studying how selectional features of lexical items function in grammatical relationships, of Freake (1962) and Southworth (1967) in studying hierarchical systems in lexis, of Halliday (1967) in analysis of the cognitive and situational options available to speakers, and of Mathiot (1967, 1968) and Garvin, Brewer and Mathiot (1967), in the semantic analysis of lexis and the cognitive study of language hold out several new approaches which may be adaptable to the investigation or restricted and elaborated coding.[2] Such investigation in relation to the Caribbean language Creole continuum is an urgent task, in view of the rapid changes being attempted by means of education in a society where the relationship between language and social class is so significant.

Notes

1. The term refers to the English-speaking territories colonized by the British as opposed to the French or Spanish Caribbean territories.In this article, the term "English-official Caribbean" is used to signify the English-speaking territories and the terms "Caribbean English Creoles" or "English-based Creoles" to refer to the Creole English language varieties discussed.
2. The work of John Rickford on African American Vernacular English contains relevant discussion on the similarity between that variety and the Caribbean English Creoles which definitely had an impact on the development of AAVE.

Appendix

A very short, selected list of Standard English features and the stratification of these that was apparent for two sets of Jamaican learners is shown in (17), where the plus sign within a column under the heading Stratification … indicates the stratification-class occupied by the relevant Standard English feature. Each pair of contrasts in 17 (i) to (iv) is meant to be taken as a unit of knowledge possessed by the speaker of Standard English, so that each pair is regarded as a single feature occupying a place in the stratification. 17 (v) and (vi) give examples of phrase-structure combinations which are meant to be taken in the same sense as the examples preceding. The first set of learners, consisting of 7-year-old children are some of the subjects in the experiment outlined in this article; the second set consists of an illustrative, typical class of training college students taught by myself in 1963. From (17) it is possible to observe the stratification for each set of learners separately and also to observe the changes attributable to the process of education and age-differences between younger and older learners. On the whole, progress in education and in age leads to a movement from D towards A within the stratification; it will be shown subsequently that this same movement occurs in the individual learner over a period of time and is not just a phenomenon observable between different groups.

(17)

Examples of standard features (Note: con. = 'in contrast with')	Rural children in the first grade of primary school at age 7 years				1st-year teacher training college students, with local educational qualifications only at age 18–20 years			
	Stratification of features as in illusuation (6)							
	A	B	C	D	A	B	C	D
(i) { /(r)st / con. /s/ } /Vowel — { /nd/ con. /n/ }			+		+	—	—	—
(ii) (a) 'I' con. 'me'	+	—	—	—	+	—	—	—
(b) 'me' con. 'my'	+	—	—	—	+	—	—	—
(c) 'John' con. 'John's'	+	—	—	—	+	—	—	—
(iii) { 'who' 'which' } con. 'waht'			+	—	+	—	—	—
(iv) [PRESENT con. PAST]/-Verb (a) PAST → { Affix /d/, /t/ } (b) { Internal change }	+	—	—	—	+	—	—	—
			+		+	—	—	—
(v) (a) AUX → PAST + Modal + 'have' + en			+		+	—	—	—
(b) NP → Pre-Art. + Art. + Adj. + Noun	+	—	—	—	+	—	—	—
(vi) (a) S₁ → The man liveø in the tree	+	—	—	—	+	—	—	—
(b) S₂ → The man* stealø meø FOOD	+ *—	—	—	—	+	—	—	—
(c) S₃ → The S₁ + man PAST + come + ↘ T-adjectivalization + PLACE + TIME + PURPOSE + S₂— T-Purpose Infinitive ← Example: The man living in the tree came here yesterday to steal my food.'			+		+	—	—	—

* Indicates that the particular lexical item is responsible for the position occupied by the whole combination in the stratification. Creole/tiif/ = 'steal'.

(18)

	Samples	Standard compared	Level of error	significance
Criterion (i)	E_1/E_{10}	0.647/0.140	0.130	0.01
	E_2/E_{20}	0.666/0.200	0.115	0.01
	E_3/E_{30}	0.630/0.186	0.163	0.02
	E_4/E_{40}	0.347/0.164	0.111	0.10 (not)
	C_1/C_{10}	0.586/0.480	0.093	Not
Criterion (ii)	E_1/E_{10}	0.621/0.011	0.089	0.01
	E_2/E_{20}	0.196/0.032	0.085	0.05
	E_3/E_{30}	0.628/0.112	0.171	0.01
	E_4/E_{40}	0.299/0	0.128	0.05
	C_1/C_{10}	0.250/0.326	0.084	Not
Criterion (iii)	E_1/E_{10}	2.78/4.91	0.75	0.01
	E_2/E_{20}	3.48/5.15	0.53	0.01
	E_3/E_{30}	2.92/4.40	0.62	0.05
	E_4/E_{40}	4.95/5.30	0.91	Not
	C_1/C_{10}	4.27/4.48	0.42	Not
Criterion (iv)	E_1/E_{10}	31.5/ 53.6	8.99	0.05
	E_2/E_{20}	24.1/ 70.6	12.21	0.01
	E_3/E_{30}	21.0/ 50.8	10.49	0.01
	E_4/E_{40}	50.6/114.9	25.75	0.05
	C_1/C_{10}	48.8/ 42.0	8.34	Not

References

Bailey, Beryl. 1962. *A Language Guide to Jamaica*. New York: Research Institute for the Study of Man.

———. 1964. "Some problems involved in the language teaching situation in Jamaica". In *Social Dialects and Language Learning*, ed. Roger Shuy, pp. 105–11. Champaign, IL: National Council of Teachers of English.

———. 1966. *Jamaican Creole Syntax*. Cambridge: Cambridge University Press.

———. [1968]. "Jamaican Creole: can dialect boundaries be defined". Paper presented at the Conference on pidginization and creolization, Mona, April 1968.

Bernstein, Basil. 1961. "Social structure, language and learning". *Educational Research* 8 (3): 163–76.

———. 1962a. "Linguistic codes, hesitation phenomena and intelligence". *Language and Speech* 5: 31–46.

———. 1962b. "Social class, linguistic codes and grammatical elements". *Language and Speech* 5: 221–40.

———. 1964. "Family role system, socialization and communication". Paper presented at Conference on Cross cultural research, University of Chicago.

———. 1965. "A socio-linguistic approach to learning". In *Social Science Survey*, ed. J. Gould. London: Pelican.

———. 1966. "Elaborated and restricted codes, an outline". In *Explorations in Sociolinguistics*, ed. S. Lieberson, *Sociological Inquiry* 36: 254–61.

Cassidy, F. 1961. *Jamaica Talk*. New York: Macmillan.

Cassidy, F., and R. Le Page. 1967. *A Dictionary of Jamaican English*. Cambridge: Cambridge University Press.

Chomsky, Noam. 1965. *Aspects of the Theory of Syntax*. Cambridge, MA: MIT Press.

Craig, Dennis, R. 1966. "Teaching English to Jamaican Creole speakers". *Language Learning* 16 (1–2).

———. 1967a. "Some early results of learning a second dialect". *Language Learning* 17 (3–4).

———. 1967b. "An experiment in teaching English". Mona, University of the West Indies, Institute of Education.

DeCamp, David. [1968]. "A generative anaylsis of the post-Creole continuum". Paper presented at the Conference on pidginization and creolization of languages, Mona, April 1968.

Frake, C.O. 1962. "The ethnographic study of cognitive systems". In *Anthropology and Human Behavior*, ed. T. Gladwin and W.C. Sturtevant, 72–85.Washington, DC: Anthropological Society of Washington.

Fries, C.C. 1963. *Teaching and Learning English as a Foreign Language*. Ann Arbor: University of MichiganPress.

Garvin, Paul, J. Brewer, and M. Mathiot. 1967. "Prediction-typing". *Language* 43 (2), pt. 2.

Halliday, M.A.K. 1967. "Notes on transitivity and theme in English". *Journal of Linguistics* 3 (1–2).

Hornby, A.S. 1950. "The situational approach in language teaching". In *Teaching English as a Second Language*, ed. H.B. Allen. New York: McGraw-Hill.

Hymes, Dell. 1966. "Two types of linguistic relativity". In *Sociolinguistics*, ed. W. Bright, pp. 114–158. The Hague: Mouton.

Katz, J.J., and J.A. Fodor 1964. "The structure of a semantic theory". In *The Structure of Language*, ed. J.A. Fodor and J.J. Katz. Englewood Cliffs, NJ: Prentice-Hall.

Labov, William. 1963. "The social motivation of a sound change". *Word* 19: 273–309.

———. 1964. "Stages in the acquisition of English in New York City". In *Social Dialects and Language Learning*, ed. by Roger Shuy. Champaign, IL: National Council of Teachers of English.

———. 1966. *The Social Stratification of English in New York City*. Washington, DC: Center for Applied Linguistics.

Lawton, David. 1963. "Social class differences in language development". *Language and Speech* 7: 182–204.

Le Page, Robert.1957–58. "General outlines of Creole English in the British Caribbean". *Orbis* 6: 373–91; 7: 54–64.

Le Page, R. and D. DeCamp. 1960. "Jamaican Creole" (*Creole Language Studies* 1, pt. 2). New York, Macmillan.

Mathiot, Madeleine. 1967. "The place of the dictionary in linguistic description". *Language* 43: 703–24.

———. 1968. *An Approach to the Cognitive Study of Language* (Publication of the Research Center in Anthropology, Folklore, and Linguistics). Bloomington: Indiana University.

Robinson, W.P. 1965. "The elaborated code in working class language". *Language and Speech* 8 (4): 243–52.

Southworth, Franklin, C. 1967. "A model of semantic structure". *Language* 43: 342–61.

Stewart, W.A. (ed.) 1964. *Non-Standard Speech and the Teaching of English*. Washington, DC: Center for Applied Linguistics.

2 | Bidialectal Education
Creole and Standard in the West Indies

1. The Definition and Location of Bidialectal Situations

A bidialectal educational situation can be considered to exist where the natural language of children differs from the standard language aimed at by schools, but is at the same time sufficiently related to this standard language for there to be some amount of overlap at the level of vocabulary and grammar. Obviously, the amount of such overlap can be expected to vary with different situations. In some cases, the two forms of speech might possess sufficient common characteristics in phonology, lexis, and syntax for them to be mutually intelligible; at the other extreme, the relatedness of the two might be insufficient to produce mutual intelligibility in continuous speech, though some commonality of lexis might still be evident to speakers in the latter case, so a bidialectal situation would approach very closely a genuinely "bilingual" one.

Many of the Caribbean countries where Creole languages are spoken do not possess educational situations that may be regarded as bidialectal in the sense just stated since, in some of these countries, the Creole language bears no relationship to the standard language used or aimed at in schools. The latter is the case, for example in different places within the officially Dutch Caribbean territories where Papiamentu (which is Spanish/Portuguese-based), Sranan (which is English-based) or Saramaccan (which is also English-based) are some of the

Creole languages. In the latter territories, the educational situation in the context of Creole language has to be regarded as clearly bilingual.

Somewhat different from, though still relatively close to situations like the latter are those existing in French Caribbean countries such as Haiti and Martinique. In those countries, the base of the Creole is the same language that is accepted as the official standard and language of education: French. At the lexical level therefore there is a considerable relationship between Creole and Standard. Despite this, however, the phonological, morphological and syntactic differences between the two forms of speech are wide enough to render them mutually unintelligible. There is some evidence, as discussed in Valdman (1969) for example, that in urban areas particularly, the occurrence of diglossia and the development of forms of speech intermediate between Creole and Standard might in time produce a situation equivalent to a bidialectal one; but at the present time, in the absence of large proportions of speakers whose habitual speech bridges the structural gap between Creole and Standard, the officially French-speaking Caribbean countries, have to be regarded, like the Dutch countries, as giving rise to educational situations that are more bilingual than bidialectal.

In the officially English-speaking territories of the Caribbean, however, where English-based Creoles either existed at some time in the past or still exist, processes of diglossia and the development of intermediate language varieties between Creole and Standard have proceeded much further than they have in the case of Haiti and Martinique just mentioned. In some of these officially English-speaking territories, as in the case of Trinidad and St Vincent, for example, the original and extreme form of an English-based Creole has all but disappeared, and what remains are systems of linguistic items intermediate between Creole and Standard. DeCamp (1971) referred to such systems as the post-Creole speech continuum. The presence of this continuum led Stewart (1962) to suggest that the Creoles of Jamaica, Guyana, Belize and the non-standard speech of the other officially English-Speaking Caribbean territories may best be treated as regional varieties or dialects of English.

It can thus be seen that there is some justification for regarding the officially English-speaking Caribbean countries as giving rise to bidialectal educational situations in a way in which the other countries do not; but it has to be noted that this difference between the officially English-speaking countries and countries like Haiti, for example, is one of degree rather than of kind. What has happened is that sociolinguistic history has caused countries like Jamaica and Guyana (both officially English-speaking) to have larger proportions of their populations speaking a language intermediate between Creole and Standard than Haiti has; but both of the former countries, however, still have considerable proportions of speakers whose habitual English-based Creole is just as incomprehensible to English ears as Haiti's French-based Creole is to French ears; and most of the remaining officially English-speaking countries, although they have no discrete Creoles like those of Jamaica or Guyana, possess just as complex a range of continuum variation.

The officially English-speaking countries that give rise to bidialectal educational situations involving Creole and Standard language in the way so far explained have a total population of about five million speakers and are as follows: the Caribbean mainland territories of Guyana and Belize, together with the islands of Jamaica, Trinidad and Tobago, Grenada, Barbados, St Vincent, St Lucia, Dominica, Monsterrat, St Kitts, Nevis, Anguilla, Antigua, the Virgin Islands, the Cayman Islands, the Turks and Caicos Islands, and the Bahamas. Some of the islands mentioned, notably St Lucia, Dominica, and Grenada, have significant proportions of their populations who speak a French Creole exclusively or both a French and an English Creole.

In these countries, the monolingual speakers of Creole or Creole-influenced language, as will be further discussed subsequently, can be estimated to form about 70% to 80% of the total speakers. These Creole or Creole-influenced monolinguals would have a language that ranges from a basilect Creole to a mesolectal language intermediate between Creole and English. A social-class classification would put most of them within the levels of lower-working, working and lower-middle class. The language-education problem that they pose is experienced mainly in the public system of primary, all age, and post-primary schools for which the governments of the respective countries are responsible.

2. The Neglect and Rediscovery of Creole

One characteristic of educational policy in the countries mentioned is that, traditionally, Creole or Creole-influenced language has been treated in schools as if it did not exist, or as if it should be eradicated if it existed. One reason for the development of this attitude to Creole is to be found in the relationship, already mentioned, between Creole and Standard at the lexical level; because of this relationship, it was easy for educational planners in the past to feel that Creole was merely a debased form of the standard language, and that this debasement could be corrected merely by a sustained exercise of carefulness on the part of the learner. The fact that this attitude is caused by the apparent lexical relationship between Creole and Standard seems proved by the more favourable attitude towards Creole found in territories where there is no relationship between Creole and Standard. The favourable attitude towards Creole in the officially Dutch-speaking territories, is attested to for example in Stewart (1962: 53), as compared with both the officially French and English-speaking territories where the attitude tends to be the opposite.

Another reason for the traditional educational attitude of neglecting Creole or Creole-influenced language or attempting to eradicate it is to be found in historical factors. Stewart (1967) comments on some of these historical factors and shows that, by the seventeenth century, all the present-day distinctive features of Creole and Creole-influenced English had already developed in the Western hemisphere and that in the officially English-speaking territories especially, it was easy for the whites to consider Creole English to be "broken" or "corrupt" English and evidence of the supposed mental limitations of the black slave population. The historian Edward Long, for example, writing of Jamaica in 1744 pointed out that "the language of the Creoles is bad English larded with the Guinea dialect", and this was obviously the pervading opinion, relevant to all the English-official Caribbean territories, which was handed down over the next two centuries. After the abolition of slavery in the 1830s the British Government made some attempt over the next century to develop public systems of education within the territories of the region, and early educational reports on the Caribbean region as a whole, like the 1938 Latrobe Reports for example, occasionally mention the role of English as a unifying force between the diverse language groups: aboriginals and Africans, French, Spanish, and Dutch speakers; and after the middle of the century Chinese, Indians, and other speakers who had come into the region. But Creole or Creole-influenced language as such was never regarded as one of the foreign languages to be reckoned with, except that in territories like St Lucia and Dominica, where speakers of French Creole were to be found, the reports of the educational officials sometimes showed concern over the French Creole problem.

It was not until the 1940s at the earliest that the problem of English in what was essentially a bidialectal educational situation (although at that time it still was not recognized as such) began to receive some attention. An example of such attention, which comes from Jamaica, but which is relevant to all the similar officially English-speaking Caribbean territories is to be seen in the report of the educational commission under L.L. Kandel (1946) which endorsed the viewpoint expressed by the Norwood Committee (1943) in Britain that there was need for alarm over the deficiencies of school-leavers' English. The Kandel report then pointed out that the need for alarm was even greater in Jamaica as there was a much more serious problem than that being experienced in Britain. Even at this relatively late period, however, the dominant attitude of schools towards Creole or Creole-influenced language continued to tend either towards ignoring it or towards eradicating it by forbidding children to speak it within the hearing of teachers; the child was invariably made to understand that his speech in school has to be "good" English.

This continued denial in the first half of the present century of the linguistic existence of the majority of Caribbean English speakers in the officially English-speaking territories occurred despite the fact that by the end of the 1920s, apart from general works on Creole like those of Van Name (1870), Schuchardt (1882–91), and the bibliography of Gaidoz (1881), there had been several studies and language collections, some going back to the previous century, and referring specifically to the officially English-speaking territories. These works are exampled in the writings of Russell (1868) relative to Jamaica; Brxonkhurst (1888), Cruickshank (1916), Scoles (1885), and Van Sertima (1897, 1905) relative to Guyana; Cruickshank (1911) relative to Barbados, and Innis (1910, 1993) and Thomas (1869) relative to Trinidad. Conditions in the remaining territories would have been closely similar to those represented in these works.

In the relevant countries, however, independent of and despite the educational system, there were factors at work that at the present time can be seen as contributing to a gradually more favourable attitude towards Creole and Creole-influenced speech. Such speech had long become codified in folk tales and vernacular humour, song and drama. In many territories, the daily and weekly newspapers (the only frequent reading for a majority of the literate population) had found it attractive, for many years, to present, written "in the dialect" (i.e., in Creole or near-Creole language) regular humorous and satirical commentaries on daily local life. Within contemporary memory some examples of the latter, under their newspaper column-titles or writers' pseudonyms are Quow, Uncle Stapie (Guyana), Macaw, Boysie (Trinidad), Quashie (Jamaica), Lizzie and Joe (Barbados, Montserrat), Annie and Josephine (Grenada), and Chatty and Papsy (Nevis). This popular interest in the vernacular culminated in the late 1940s, at the same time as the first expressions of educational alarm (referred to above) over English language proficiency, in a growing number of Creole language collections and commentaries like, for example, some of Louise Bennett's publications in Jamaica (e.g., Bennett, 1942, 1943, 1950) Frank Collymore's serializations of "Words and phrases of Barbadian dialect" (e.g., Collymore 1952), and in Guyana in a series of articles on aspects of Creole language by D.A. Westmas and Richard Allsopp, respectively, in the journal *Kyk-Over-All* between 1948 and 1953.

This growth of popular literacy interest in Creole might have had, by itself, some influence on attitudes in education, but in any case it was followed closely by another, probably inevitable development which is the one that really made some educational change imperative. This development referred to is the beginning of modern grammatical studies of Creoles in the officially English-speaking territories.

Some of the first results of such studies are to be seen in Taylor (1945, 1952, 1955, 1961, 1963, 1968), Le Page (1952, 1955, 1957; ed., 1959), Bailey (1953, 1962, 1966), Allsopp (1958a and b, 1962), Le Page and DeCamp (1960), Cassidy (1961), Alleyne (1961, 1963), and Cassidy and Le Page (1967). This body of work includes descriptions of the phonology, lexis and grammar of Dominica and Jamaican Creoles, some aspects of the morphology and syntax of Guyanese Creole, consideration of some sociolinguistic factors in relation to St Lucia and Jamaica, some early thoughts on how language studies in the English-official Caribbean might be further promoted, and some general descriptive comments on Caribbean Creoles not yet substantially dealt with.

In this work, Jamaican Creole gets the most comprehensive treatment in terms of its syntax, lexicology, and segmental phonology. Obviously, most of the relevant English-official Caribbean territories that have been earlier listed here received no attention in these studies and, apart from the work on Jamaica, no one country received any wide-ranging study. Nevertheless, the work cited here was very significant for the Caribbean region as a whole because firstly it created a scientific framework within which interested persons involved with language in the region could observe linguistic facts in the territories to which the work referred; secondly, it permitted such persons to make comparisons, within this scientific framework, between linguistic facts as described in this work and facts as known, merely through informal experience, relevant to territories not yet formally studied. As a result of this work, and the possibility just mentioned to which it gave rise, it became possible for educators within the region to view English-official Caribbean language-education problems in a manner comparable to how problems of bilingualism or multilingualism might be viewed in contemporary times; although the existence of this possibility does not necessarily imply its actual realization or achievement.

Work such as the preceding has continued up to the present, with some of the more recent additions to it taking on increasingly theoretical forms: Bailey (1971), for example, suggested that distinctions might be drawn between

basilectal and mesolectal forms of Creole by measuring the quantity and complexity of the transformational rules that separated the respective forms from
both Standard English and basilect Creole; and DeCamp (1971) showed that
linguistic forms in the continuum between Creole and Standard were not just
an ordered collection among which speakers shifted in response to social situations, but that the forms of the continuum were implicationally linked, so
that the presence of specific forms rendered certain others obligatory. Subsequently, following the work of Labov (e.g., 1971) and C.J. Bailey (e.g., 1969,
1970) in Hawaii, Bickerton (1971, 1971a, 1972, 1972a, 1973) pursued further
implications of DeCamp's thesis and suggested that in the Caribbean English
Creole continuum, as presumably also universally in all speech communities,
variation within and between idiolects existed as sets of implicationally linked
characteristics that could not be described by static grammatical models. The
developments apparent in these studies, contribute to grammatical theory generally as well as to knowledge of Creole language situations of the bidialectal
or multidialectal type; the implications of these developments for bidialectal
education will be considered subsequently.

Concurrently with these developments, and additional to work appearing
in Hymes (ed., 1971), there have been several studies within the West Indies,
some of them unpublished, that describe specific aspects of English-based Creole or mesolectal language and thereby contribute further to the kind of information that the educator needs for work in relevant situations; among the latter
studies are the following: Carrington (1967, 1969), Allsopp (1965), Reisman
(1961, 1965), Hughes (1966), Lawton, D.L. (1963, 1964, 1971), Solomon (1966),
Christie (1969), Warner (1967), and Winford (1972); in addition, a collection
of papers currently in preparation for publication (Craig, ed., forthcoming)
includes some relevant additional writing of Berry, Cassidy, Spears, Edwards,
Allsopp, and Solomon (see references) that is of a descriptive or theoretical linguistic kind, as well as some other work of educational relevance that will be
mentioned subsequently. The descriptive and theoretical writings just cited add
the following information to that provided by the earliest set of Creole language
studies already mentioned: additional information on the lexis and phonology
of Jamaican, Cayman, Barbadian, and Guyanese Creoles (Cassidy, Lawton,
Berry, Allsopp, Spears); information on the distribution and structure of French
Creole in St Lucia and Dominica (Carrington, Christie); tentative and very general statements on the linguistic and sociolinguistic situation in Belize (Allsopp
1965), Antigua (Reisman), and Grenada (Hughes); information on the syntactic
structure of Creole and post-Creole language and the socio-linguistic situation

in Trinidad (Warner, Winford, Solomon), and Guyana (Edwards). This work is not even in quality, and there is no comprehensive survey of the region as a whole, but it is sufficient to show the distribution of Creole and mesolectal language, the general nature of the language system in most territories, and some more detailed treatment of one or two situations sufficient to permit a degree of extrapolation to other situations where adequate work has not yet been done.

3. The Use of the Vernacular in Education

Growth of knowledge about Creole language situations, such as that outlined above for the Caribbean Creole-English situation, coincided with the growth of new nations in the Third World and an international recognition of the need for these new nations to have educational systems that would be fully relevant in each case to the specific national identity, environment, and goals; part of this recognition implied the need for each child to receive at least his earliest education in the language that was most natural to him: his mother tongue. In the light of this recognition, the fiction, maintained for over a century, that Standard English was the mother tongue of Caribbean Creole-speaking or Creole-influenced children could no longer be maintained. One of the first concrete reactions to this recognition was the proposal that the Creole or mesolectal language-speaking children, in officially English-speaking Caribbean territories should be used as the language of primary, even if for no other, education. An early example of such suggestion is to be seen in the UNESCO (1953) monograph on the use of vernacular languages in education, where it was suggested that some of the officially English-speaking territories in the Caribbean were among the areas of the world where Creole languages might well be used in Education. Up to the present, however, more than five decades after this suggestion, most of these territories have not attempted to implement it.

The chief reason why the Creole or Creole-influenced language of Caribbean Creole English-speaking children has not been used in education lies in deep-seated community attitudes to Creole. As referred to previously, the old official attitude of ignoring its existence or advocating its eradication has already been mentioned. In the community at large, Creole language has generally been identified historically with slavery, and in more recent times with very low social status and lack of education. This feeling about Creole exists even in the minds of its speakers, most of whom would attempt, if they could, to modify their speech in direction of Standard English in the presence of an English Speaker, and would feel insulted if a stranger who is obviously non-Creole-speaking attempts to converse with them in Creole. In this context, even the most Creole-speaking of parents tend to regard Standard English as the language of social mobility, and would tend to think that anyone who suggests the use of Creole and Creole-influenced language in education is advocating the socio-economic repression of the masses. This attitude of Creole and Creole-influenced speakers towards English has been mentioned in Bailey (1964) with reference to Jamaica, but it is an attitude that is to be found in all the officially English-speaking Caribbean countries. It is not any way unique to these countries however, as it is very similar to that attitude of non-Standard speakers in the USA which Wolfram (1970: 29) describes, and which has been responsible for the non-acceptance of dialect readers in some "black" English communities. Obviously, it is an attitude that can be expected in any situation which is essentially bidialectal in its nature, although there are some genuinely bilingual situations. Rickford, Smitherman and other researchers in the US when dealing with the question of 'ebonics' or the non-standard dialect spoken by blacks, have also come up against similar attitudes to these mentioned among Caribbean and Central American bidialectal communities.

In effect it is an attitude that represents a type of socio-psychological dualism in which the low-status language is stubbornly preserved by its speakers as a part of their identity and cultural integrity, but at the same time these very speakers resist any measures which, by extending the societal role of their own low-status language, might impede their children's acquisition of the accepted high-status language. At the base of the attitude is probably the very pragmatic realization that it is unlikely that the high-status language could ever be completely replaced, and that even if it is, its status in the wider world would still make it a very desirable acquisition.

Another very important reason why Creole or Creole-influenced language has not been used in education within officially English-speaking territories is to be found in the technical difficulties that would be involved. One such difficulty would be that of the standardization of the phonology and grammar of the non-Standard language and the choice of an orthography for it. It is possible, in the matter of phonology and orthography, that if the language of a territory is of a mesolectal kind without the existence of a basilectal Creole, then solutions to the problem might be similar to those suggested in Stewart (1969) and Fasold (1969) for American black dialects where conventional English orthography is retained.

In the latter cases, English orthography represents the underlying realities of the non-Standard "dialects" to such an extent that it is easily possible to use the same orthography and incidentally benefit from having a single writing system for all speakers. However, in cases like those of Jamaica and Guyana, where there are basilect Creoles departing farther from English than mesolectal language does, the use of an English orthography might be somewhat more problematical, especially when relationships between phonology and grammar are taken into consideration although it would be possible for teachers to use English spellings and permit a wide range of variant speech renditions as has been suggested DeCamp (1972).

In the matter of standardizing Creole or Creole-influenced grammar, there are still larger problems, however, occasioned by the range of continuum variation to which persons have become accustomed, and the difficulty of deciding on the point of the continuum at which the standard grammar will be selected. The selection of the basilect Creole would exclude most mesolectal speakers, and the selection of a mesolect would not solve the most serious societal problems of Creole speakers; an idea of the extent of the problem can easily be gauged by an examination of the wide variation that is possible in the Creole and Creole-influenced versions of Standard English sentences in Craig (1971a: 374). There have been suggestions and recommendations in several of the English-official Caribbean territories, including Barbados which is problematic because of the move away from basilectal to more mesolectal varieties, but the standardization of such varieties will continue to remain a very difficult issue to address.

Assuming, however, that the linguistic, technical problems just mentioned can be overcome, there are problems of implementation and costs of action programmes of the kind discussed in Bull (1955), that would by themselves tend to induce governments to avoid the use of Creole or Creole-influenced language in education. First of all, in the officially English-speaking territories relevant here, it would be necessary for a relatively large percentage (probably about 50%) of the professional people working in education to be taught the vernacular that is to be used. Textbooks and other educational materials would then need to be prepared in the vernacular in a situation where persons with the requisite skills would even in normal circumstances be very scarce. Even if the use of the vernacular is confined to primary education, with the prestige language being introduced subsequently as a second language and used later as the language of instruction in secondary school, the financial cost, to a newly developing territory, of the measures just mentioned would be enormous and, except in the absence of a viable and nationally respectable alternative, quite likely prohibitive.

Apart from all this, a country with the bidialectal type of Creole-language situation that is relevant here would need to consider seriously whether the use of the low-prestige language in the public system of schools and at a low level of education might not accentuate social divisions within the society rather than remove them, especially in a context where most children already attend primary schools and acquire some amount at least of mesolectal language, and where there is a selective system of secondary schools geared to the production of an educated elite. It is obvious that these considerations would not apply with equal force in all territories with bidialectal situations, and might not apply at all even in those Creole-speaking countries which approach the bidialectal type very closely (like Haiti, for example, where the relatively small proportion of children completing primary education and the 90% use of Creole within the society render such considerations inoperative). In the officially English-speaking Caribbean territories, however, these considerations do apply and, together with what has already been said above about community attitudes, explain why governments have never seriously considered using the vernacular in education.

4. Teaching the Standard by Correction

When the educational use of Creole or Creole-influenced language is ruled out in a bidialectal situation such as the English-official Caribbean one, the most obvious alternative is for schools to employ a teaching strategy based on getting children to correct those characteristics of their own speech that differ from the language aimed at by schools. These are the characteristics which, in traditional school terminology would be regarded as resulting in language "errors" or "mistakes", and which the applied linguist would regard as contrasts between the native and target languages. The problem with this strategy of correction is that it leaves the learners completely at the mercy of the ad hoc and occasional intervention of the teacher, puts them in the position where they can learn only after they have made what they often come to regard as embarrassing mistakes, and invariably makes them so aware of the possibility of mistakes that they become afraid and often incapable of expressing themselves in formal situations. In the older examples of the application of this strategy, some teaching of traditional English grammar would have formed a part of the classroom procedures, and in some ways this grammatical teaching was not altogether worthless, when carried out by intelligent teachers, as it gave the non-Standard speakers some logical framework within which they could systematize the "corrections" that they learned, and within which they could see the Standard language as a whole; there is no denying, however, that in many, probably a majority of cases, learners acquired merely a rote knowledge of one or two inaccurate grammatical rules which in no way affected their ability to express themselves in formal situations.

The later work by Pollard, *From Jamaican Creole to Standard English,* also suggests a comparative approach between the two varieties but does so in a creative way, setting out valuable activities which can be used in the classroom to make the comparative approach more meaningful to students.

With the gradual popularization of modern linguistics and demonstration by teachers and scholars like C.C. Fries (e.g., 1940, 1952) that traditional grammatical rules often misrepresented English as it is actually spoken, and also with a better understanding, through child development studies (see, e.g., Carroll, 1969), of how language is learned, the teaching of "grammar" has declined in schools. However, present day survivals of the strategy of language-teaching by correction, with or without traditional grammar, can still be found in bidialectal classroom situations in the English-official Caribbean as well as elsewhere; in the USA, for example, not so long ago, Crow et al. (1966: 124) showed the survival of this strategy when they stated:

> Some of the causes of speech problems of the socially disadvantaged children are similar to those of listening. For example, a deficiency in auditory discrimination may result from the failure of parents to correct mistakes in spoken language, owing either to lack of knowledge of correct speech or to sheer indifference. Faulty auditory discrimination can be illustrated by the child's confusing the "th" sound with the "f" sound in a word such as "Mother" for which he may say "Muffer". Correct speech is learned through imitation in the home and elsewhere. Many parents of socially disadvantaged children do not realize that their speech is incorrect and that their children's poor speech patterns are formed in the home. In the school, corrective help is given, but the time is too short for much progress, and when the child returns home, he is confronted with the inferior speech.

Like all advocates of a teaching-by-correction strategy, the writers of this extract make no use of the concept that low-social-status speech is, for all practical purposes, a dialect with its own distinctive rules of phonology and grammar and that the problem of learning standard speech is that of learning a new dialect. However, the importance of the home environment is well recognized, and it is precisely because of this environment that the strategy of teaching by correction inevitably fails, since that strategy has within it no way of systematically teaching sets of new language structures in such a way that they have a reasonable chance of persisting parallel to the language of the home.

In the officially English-speaking Caribbean, first in Jamaica and from there to other territories, a movement away from the correction strategy began in the late 1950s. It is well illustrated in this extract from Walters (1958), which it will be noted appeared fully eight years before Crow (et al.) already cited.

> The general attitude to this problem has been that Jamaican Creole structure is wrong and must be corrected. Training College syllabuses in English have begun the first and second year courses with "Correction of common errors in speech", and "A more formal application of the rules of grammar to common errors in English in Jamaican", while the Code For Elementary Schools does say: "Spontaneity should not be discouraged by correction in the early stages" (Code of Regulations of the Education Department, 1938). A Training College principal recently announced, in a public discussion – "There is only one answer to the question of dialect – that is, it has no place whatever in our elementary schools", and a similar statement was circulated, in another territory, by the Inspector of Schools to all teachers. This attitude, that local speech is wrong and must not be allowed, held so firmly by educators and implemented in schools, has certainly had little effect on local speech, save to inhibit the spontaneous speech and writing in schools and produce a stilted and artificial style in the "educated".
>
> A gradual change of attitude is being noted, however, as above when teachers are warned not to begin corrections too early and stifle spontaneity. A further step takes us away from the concept of "correcting wrong speech", towards learning a new way of saying things. A recently distributed directive on "The Curriculum of Primary And Post Primary Schools" states: "The Jamaican vernacular is not the great obstacle to learning English it is generally supposed to be. It is a bridge to be used by the teacher to get to the use of the English language. There might well be the tacit understanding in our schools that English is the language spoken and written, but the Jamaican vernacular is understood." A revised syllabus for Jamaican Primary Schools suggests – "Interest must be aroused in speaking correct English as soon as possible, not as a matter of correcting what is wrong, but as acquiring new skill."

Enlightened as this change obviously was on the question of the "correction" strategy, it did not however, and probably could not at that point in time, have within it an understanding of all the linguistic realities that would have made a systematic approach to the language and reading problem fully possible. The approach then advocated was an "experience" approach which would get children to hear "new ways of saying things", induce them to say things in these new ways, and get them to read and write the new language. What was lacking in this approach was an orderly structure for the children's acquisition and production of the new language; by it, children came into contact with the new language fortuitously and at odd moments, just as they would in a completely first-language, or mother-tongue, educational situation and there were no procedures within the advocated approach whereby the patterns and structures of the new language could be learned in such a way as not to be suppressed by the dominant home-language environment.

5. Teaching the Standard Langauge as a Second Dialect

As has been pointed out already, the growth of Creole language studies in the officially English-speaking Caribbean after 1950 brought forcibly to people's attention the fact that Standard English, if not actually a foreign language, was clearly in the nature of a second dialect to most Caribbean English speakers. One result of this awareness can be seen in the appearance in the English-official Caribbean of a number of writings which looked in various ways at the language-education problem and made suggestions about alleviating it. Including Walters (1958) already cited, the earliest of these language-educational studies were concerned with documenting what happened when Creole-influenced individuals at different levels of education attempted to receive and produce English, both in speech and writing. A statement of some of these is to be found in the Faculty of Education (1965) Report of the conference on linguistics, language teaching and the teaching of English, convened at the University of the West Indies. Some of these studies, like those of Craig (1964) and Grant (1964), were not system descriptive in a linguistic sense, but were concerned with error analyses, occurrence frequencies of various types of linguistic items and the comparisons that could be made, in these terms, between different social-class types and age-groups of learners.

Studies of this kind seem useful for the planning of language-education in the region for several reasons. Firstly, in the context of the Creole/Standard continuum, actual frequency distributions of specific linguistic items give a more practical picture of the competence of speakers than static system-description can alone and by itself; secondly, there is the pragmatic educational necessity for teachers to be able to compare different types of learners and to perceive quantitative as well as qualitative language differences where these occur; and thirdly, in the absence of language development and performance data relevant to the officially English-speaking Caribbean, of the kind that can be found relevant to other societies, well evaluated and summarized in sources like Carroll (1960) and Denis Lawton (1968), for example, studies of this kind seem well justified in the circumstances of the officially English-speaking Caribbean.

Additional to the preceding, there began to appear at this time (in the early 1960s) several analyses of the classroom implications of Creole language-studies, indications of the quasi-foreign language nature of the language situation, and general suggestions for necessary teaching programmes in Caribbean schools. Similar work has continued to appear up to the present and the relevant publications are Figueroa (1962, 1972), Gray (1963), Bailey (1963), Cuffie (1964), Jones (1966), and Carrington (1968, 1970). Some very recent additions to work of this kind are to be seen in Carrington (1971), Allsopp (1972), Edwards (1972), and Solomon (1972) where the language-teaching implications of specific phonological, lexical and syntactic characteristics of Caribbean English Creole or continuum language are examined. This most recent work differs from what preceded it by having its language-teaching considerations limited in each case to some single, specific aspect of linguistic form: implicational relationships in the continuum, prosodic features, morpho-syntactic variation in items like "have" and "be", and so on. It supplements the thesis of the foreign-language or quasi-foreign language nature of the language situation by a relatively in-depth analysis of the related linguistic form in each case, and what it would mean to teach an area of the Standard language that corresponds to or is related to that aspect of linguistic form. The problems of the total content of the language programme for children, its classroom implementation, and wider educational issues such as valid goals and the strategies for achieving these are not objects of immediate concern in this work.

By the middle of the 1960s the resemblance between the Creole language situations in the officially English-speaking Caribbean and the non-Standard English problems in the United States of America had been perceived. Stewart, who in 1964 had participated in the West Indian conference responsible for the Faculty of Education (1965) Report already cited, edited in the same year the influential "Non-Standard Speech and the Teaching of English". In the latter, the Jamaican language situation received a significant treatment, and the point is strongly made that foreign language teaching methods seem necessary in the quasi-foreign language situations of Creole and other non-Standard speakers in officially English-speaking countries, including the United States of America. Appearing in the same year as the preceding, and of a similar import, was the publication *Social Dialects and Language Learning* (Shuy, ed., 1966) in which also appeared a contribution on the Jamaican situation (Bailey 1964).

It has already been shown in section three of this article that the community attitudes responsible for the failure of dialect readers in some parts of the United States of America are similar to the Caribbean attitudes that made it impracticable for the vernacular to be used as the language of instruction in schools; and in the studies just mentioned the recognition of the similarity of the second-dialect characteristics of the language situations in the USA and the English-official Caribbean much of the work done in any one is likely to have some relevance for the other. In this respect, work such as that of Labov (1964; et al, 1965, 1966, 1969). Shuy (et al. 1967), Wolfram (1969), and Fasold and Shuy (eds., 1970), which provides structural descriptions of language variation and of non-Standard speech in the USA, and which suggests ways in which such descriptions need to be taken into account in school programmes, gives an example of the kinds of factors that also apply in the officially English-speaking Caribbean; similarly, work on the teaching of reading in the context of non-Standard speech, like that of the Baratz and Shuy (1969) have corresponding import. In some instances, researchers have been done expressly with both the American and Caribbean situations in mind; this is the case, for example, in Shuy (1972) which discusses strategies for implementing sociolinguistic principles in schools and DeCamp (1972) which examines problems and possibilities in the use of Standard English books by Creole-speaking children.

In all of the work referred to in the present section of this article, as pointed out already, mention is made of the possibilities of using foreign-language teaching methods in the essentially bidialectal educational situations of the United States of America and the English-official Caaribbean. In some cases, as in Stewart (1964), mention is also made of the fact, to the relevant learners, Standard English is neither a native nor a foreign language. For a long time after the first proposals for the use of foreign language teaching methods in the relevant situations, however, there were no clear statements of the adaptations that inevitably became necessary because the native language of the learner overlapped considerably with the target, and because also, particularly in the Caribbean situation, most non-Standard speakers were capable of varying their performance along a stretch of the Creole/ Standard continuum. The methods that were advocated varied from a formal English-as-a-second-language programme, with a strictly ordered set of procedures based on contrasts between English and the basilect, to the almost informal and fortuitous counselling described by Brooks (1964):

. . . A trained volunteer now works with Carlos, often in this way. The boy picks up an interesting picture.

"I hab a tree, with leebs", says Carlos.

"Yes, you *have* a tree, with *leaves*", replies the teacher. "*Say have – leaves*".

"Have – *leaves*" replies Carlos, learning the /v/ sound in English. Because this boy already knows some English, he needs mainly to have someone take an interest in him to draw out what he knows, to involve him in the life around him, to help him share with others – orally and in writing – his valuable contributions, and *to correct some speech difficulties.*

The differences in the emphasis and focus of the various suggested applications of foreign-language teaching procedures are such that it would obviously be beneficial to have some clear theory of the relationship between foreign language teaching and what is essentially second dialect teaching. In the Caribbean, the first teaching experiment aiming at some formalization of the new methodology began in Jamaica in 1965 and has been described in Craig (1969). Some theoretical principles underlying the methodology itself have been discussed in Craig (1966a and b, 1967, 1971a). In these studies it is shown that in a bidialectal situation of the kind relevant here, the learning of the new dialect proceeds as a mixing of newly learned linguistic features with older ones not yet replaced, so that in the case of the non-Standard speaker, the growing Standard repertoire that is being learned never appears separate and distinct until after prolonged learning when the acquisition of the Standard is quite complete. At each intermediate point of learning, the Standard tends to be produced mixed with survivals of the original non-Standard dialect. This does not mean that the speaker necessarily loses his original Creole or dialect, although this could happen with prolonged immersion into the cultural environment of the (high-prestige) Standard speech; but what happens is that the speaker acquire the ability to shift his speech closer to the Standard-language end of the Creole/Standard or dialect continuum; in other words, learning of the standard proceeds as a movement along this continuum.

In some cases during the acquisition of the Standard, a continuum can actually be seen in creation where none existed before, or rather, where no continuum items of a particular kind existed before. This was noticed, for example, in some of the children (7–8 years old) considered in the teaching experiment and related studies last referred to. Before those children became subjects of a modified second-language teaching programme, they did not possess "is" and "has", and for the latter mentioned they used only the uninflected form of the verb "have". After a period of learning "is" both as copula and as AUX + "ing" – form, and before they learned to use "has", they regularly produced "is have" wherever "has" would have been appropriate. This habit passed away naturally, and without any special corrective, after children learned to use "has".

Linked to the tendency of the children here being considered to mix newly acquired forms with their original language, to proceed in this way along the dialect or Creole/ Standard continuum, and even to create a new continuum, was the ability to comprehend much more Standard language than they could produce. Wolfram (1970: 17) points out that such ability seems consistent with the viewpoint of Labov and Cohen (1967) that the main differences between non-Standard and Standard language appear to be on the surface rather than on the underlying levels of language; Labov himself (1969: 24) refers to such ability as having been significantly proved by repetition tests given to subjects in some of his earlier researches; and Baratz (1969) found a similar situation through subsequent tests of the same kind in her own work. It is significant that the evidence put forward by Labov (1969) and Baratz (1969) is that the non-Standard speakers , while being unable themselves to produce the Standard language, were able to restructure that language in non-Standard equivalents, showing indeed that it was the underlying structure that must have been comprehended.

These indications in the children in the Caribbean experiment confirmed a basic principle that directed the teaching methodology. This principle was that, as far as the learner was concerned, the continuum between Creole and Standard consisted of four hierarchical strata of linguistic structures as follows: A, those common to both Standard and non-Standard speech and therefore within the production repertoire of the learner; B, those not usually produced in the informal, non-Standard speech of the learner, but known to him and produced under stress in prestige social situations; C, those which the learner would recognize and comprehend if used by other speakers (especially in a meaningful context), but which the learner himself would be unable to produce; and D, those totally unknown to the learner. As will be shown subsequently, it is sometimes convenient to regard elements of strata A and B as forming a single class, and similarly, those of C and D as forming a single class; but even when regarded in this way the four underlying strata show that in the class of second-dialect language known already to the learner, there is a set of items which he would use only in unusual or very formal situations, and in the class of second-dialect language not within the production repertoire of the learner, there is a set of items which can be recognized and comprehended.

The special implications of this stratification of language vis-à-vis the Creole or non-Standard learner of English has been discussed in Craig (1971: 378) where it is shown that, because of the B and C strata, the learner often fails to perceive new target D elements in the teaching situation, unlike the learner of a foreign language. Consequent upon this, the reinforcement of learning which derives from the learner's satisfaction at mastering a new element, and knowing he has mastered it, is minimal, unlike that accruing to the learner of a foreign language; and because of the ease of shifting from Standard English to Creole or other non-Standard speech and vice-versa, the learner, again unlike the learner of a foreign language, resists any attempt to restrict his use of language exclusively within the new language elements being taught to him.

In the light of these implications, it is not surprising if many non-Standard speakers taught by foreign language methods continue to show a very low rate of acquiring Standard language. Kochman (1969: 87) in discussing this point, felt that the "efficiency quotient" of Standard language teaching, i.e., the result that comes from an input of time and effort, is so negligible that the wisdom of at all attempting to teach the Standard under conditions such as those relevant here has to be questioned. Usually, the reasons for such poor results have been ascribed completely to social factors and the unfavourable attitudes of learners as in, for example, Fasold (1968) and Abrahams (1970). There is no doubt that social and attitudinal factors are exceedingly important and obviously play a part, but slow or negligible acquisition of the Standard is not restricted to poorly motivated learners or to learners below the age of social awareness (vide Labov 1964: 91) at which some motivation might develop. The question therefore needs to be studied, namely whether the very nature of bidialectal situations does not produce strictly linguistic and non-attitudinal factors that have some additional bearing on the poor results of language teaching.

The teaching programme dictated by the suggested stratification of language, vis-à-vis the learner, and by the considerations related to that stratification is structured as follows:

1. Topics for treatment in language are selected so as to reflect the interests, maturity and immediate cultural environment of the learners, but at the same time so as to permit adequate use of the specific linguistic structures that form the goal of teaching at the specific point in time.
2. The learners are led by the teacher to explore the topic fully in whatever language the learners possess. The teacher may either speak the vernacular, or speak another type of language closer to the Standard or speak the Standard itself, so long as the learners are able to comprehend easily; and the teacher accepts whatever language the learners choose to respond in,

including such new language as is infiltrating into the learner's competence. This part of the programme is completely oral and may be designated "free talk". The purpose of this part is to promote normal growth
and development of the learners in whatever language medium is most
natural to them.

3. The teacher uses the selected topic, or aspects of the topic, as the basis
of systematic quasi-foreign language practice. Because of the high rate
of recognition and comprehension in the bidialectal situation, through
the learners' possession of the language strata A, B, and C, teaching
procedures do not usually call for defensive imitation drill, but rather
more for substitution and transformation practices, controlled dialogues and dramas, simulated situations geared to direct to a creative
use of the specific linguistic structures that are aimed at. This part of
the programme may be designated "controlled talk" and only Standard
language is used.

4. For teaching in (3) preceding, linguistic structures are selected so that,
relevant to the A, B, C, D classification of structures already discussed,
the learners are forced to use a target structure or target structures
selected from a fortuitous combination of C or D, and at the same time
to use incidental structures which come from a combination of A and B.

5. Language learners who are also learning to read use material consisting only of such previously learned linguistic structures at each given
stage such as at (3), and that are relevant to the topics discussed at (2).
Language learners who can already read may benefit significantly from
materials that are for their intensive use. The purpose of this set of measures is to ensure that the acquisition of and interest in reading is not
hampered by Standard-Language deficiencies, and that reading and
language-learning should reinforce each other; once reading is firmly
acquired, however, there is no longer any point in linking it to the formal
learning of language structure.

6. For all learners, use is made in writing only of those linguistic structures
that have already been learned as at (3), and in most cases the content of
the writing is restricted to topics treated as at (2). By this means, writing
is closely linked to proficiency in speech, and one reinforces the other.

7. The various subject-areas of the total school curriculum enter into the
selection of topics explained as at (1) so that aspects of these areas get
re-worked in controlled speech, reading and writing in the same way as
all other experiences.

The difference between what is outlined here and strictly foreign-language teaching procedures lies in what has been termed free talk and the way in which controlled talk, reading and writing are linked to it and to one another; the different parts of the programme have to be planned together and be well integrated. In this way, the learner gets the kind of stimulating education that ought to be present in a first-language programme, but at the same time, linked to this stimulation and arising out of it, there is a concentration on the ordered and sequenced teaching of new language elements. The built-in resistance of the second-dialect learner to such teaching is countered by the carry-over of his free-talk interests into other activities, by the constant reinforcement passing from one activity to another, and by the encouraged possibility of newly learned language gradually infiltrating into free talk, becoming a part of it and becoming gradually augmented. This last mentioned possibility is in fact more than just a possibility since it has been shown, as already discussed, to be the inevitable way in which language learning proceeds in this situation, i.e., as a gradual mixture and replacement of items along the continuum. This mixture and replacement occasioned by new language learning, as explained already, does not mean that the learners lose their original vernacular. They retain their original vernacular for such occasions as it is needed in their home and peer-group environment, but at the same time they acquire an increasing ability to shift their formal speech into the Standard-language end of the continuum until they achieve some acceptable proficiency in Standard speech.

On the way towards the achievement of such proficiency, many compromises are inevitable: some learners might persist in retaining certain of their original speech characteristics in the most nearly Standard language they learn to produce, others might achieve good native proficiency in reading and writing the Standard language but at the same time persist in their original non-Standard speech even on the most formal occasions, and so on. It does not seem that bidialectal education ought to expect more than this. Fishman and Leuders-Salmon (1972) have shown that German dialect speakers react to the necessity as well as the experiences of learning High German in some of the characteristic ways that are now well known in the United States of America and the Caribbean language situations. It would thus seem that the factors discussed here are to be found universally in many different bidialectal situations.

The principles and procedures paragraphs will not be found in uniform application in schools within the English-official Caribbean. In Jamaica, where the educational principles just discussed were first and still are being worked out, indications of the methodology will be noticed in Ministry of Education school syllabuses and guidelines for teachers where "an integrated approach" to language teaching is spoken of; the "integration" involves the components of the programme already outlined here. At the present time, an effort is being made in the Ministry's Curriculum Development Thrust to supply teachers with detailed guides and materials for teaching along the suggested lines. The ideas and procedures are also in process of being disseminated through others of the officially English-speaking Caribbean territories; in Guyana, for example, much consideration has been given to the nature of the Guyanese language situation and the needs that exist in education. The discussion has proceded very much along the general lines followed in this chapter, and some of it is exampled in Tyndal (1965, 1972), Armstrong (1968), Wilson (1968), Cave (1970, 1971) Craig (1971), and Trotman (1973). In the last mentioned territory also, the production of classroom materials incorporating the relevant procedures is in progress.

In the Eastern Caribbean, independently of the Jamaica-based work, the School of Education of the University of The West Indies together with a UNESCO curriculum development programme in that area has been working on the development of language-teaching materials with an English-as-a-second language approach. Preceding this development and continuing concurrently with it, there is in Trinidad an ongoing survey of school-children's language (Carrington and Borely 1969); there has also been concluded a survey of teaching practices (Carrington, Borely, and Knight (1972), textbooks in use in schools (Knight, Carrington, and Borley 1972) and the home-language background of Trinidad children (Carrington, Borely, and Knight 1972a); the latter collections of information are considered as a preliminary to the development of teaching procedures in that territory.

No matter what stage of development has been reached at present in the development of bidialectal educational procedures in the relevant individual English-official Caribbean territories, however, it seems quite clear that, in the long run, the fact that such procedures are necessary and are at the same time inevitably different from both native and foreign-language teaching procedures will have to be faced; it seems important that when this happens, the principles and procedures discussed above should be available for more extensive trial throughout the region.

6. Language and Social Class In a Bidialectal Situation

The speakers of Creole or non-Standard language are invariably of low social-status, therefore, in bidialectal situations of the kind relevant here, there are problems of educating economically depressed and low-status persons in a socially stratified society. Since the 1960s particularly, there has been considerable discussion of the relationships between social class, language, mental ability, and education. Much of this discussion is as relevant to bidialectal situations of the kind relevant here, the problems of educating such speakers are very much the problems of educating economically depressed and low-status persons in a socially stratified society. Since the 1960s particularly, there has been considerable discussion of the relationships between social class, language, mental ability, and education. Much of this discussion is as relevant to bidialectal education in the officially English-speaking Caribbean as it is in similar situations elsewhere, and it has been found essential that the planning of West Indian school programmes should take note of it.

By far the most important aspect of this discussion is that which emerged out of work like that of Reissman (1962) in the United States of America and Bernstein (1961a, b, c, ; 1962a, b; 1965, 1966) in Britain. The former expanded on the thesis of the limited mental and learning capacities of the "culturally deprived child"; the latter, actually preceding this in point of time, gave an apparently rational basis for this thesis by suggesting that the different patterns of socialization in lower and upper social-class environments gave rise respectively to restricted and elaborated linguistic codes, the latter code indicating a "more extensive and qualitatively different order of verbal planning" as compared with the former. The 1961 and 1962 work of Bernstein states the objective linguistic characteristics of these codes and shows that restricted code-users of low social class, as predicted, are generally lower in measured intelligence and educational achievement than elaborated code users who, as predicted, are mostly found in the upper social class.

The remainder of this work which followed in the later 1960s stressed the socialization factors somewhat more and showed that it was possible for both codes to arise in any social class depending on the conditioning received by subjects; but in any case, the dominant social-class pattern was still that demonstrated in the earlier work. The Bernstein thesis has received general support in the work of Lawton (1963, 1964, 1968), Robinson (1965; et al. 1968), Coulthard (et al. 1968), Hawkins (1969) as well as elsewhere; the main additional fact emerging from these researchers is that low social-class subjects, influenced by education, sometimes have an elaborated code available for selected purposes; but this does not alter the main thesis that on the whole, the lower social class is habituated in a mode of language use that puts it at a disadvantage in the performance of certain linguistic and intellectual operations.

This view point of low-social-class disabilities was firmly accepted in most educational programmes of the 1960s that have had to deal with social-class or cultural extremes. It is well exemplified in writings such as those of Corbin (et al. 1965), Crow (et al. 1966) and Bereiter (et al. 1966) which have had a wide influence on early educational practices not only in the United States of America but elsewhere. The main opposition to this viewpoint has come from sociolinguists; Labov (et al. 1965, 1969), for example, has shown that lower-social-class language in natural and uninhibiting circumstances is accompanied by much creativity and efficiency in the treatment of logical relationships and the processing of ideas. It is shown on the other hand that the expression of meaning in upper-social-class language can often be accompanied by much vagueness, empty verbosity and a lack of consciousness. It is also shown that the context in which upper- and lower-social-class children are studied: classroom-type situations and topics, talking about pictures, obviously upper-class interviews and testers, and so on, militate against lower-social class children who cannot help but be uncomfortable and anxious in such contexts, and who are thereby induced to minimize their language production.

But so far, apart from questioning the circumstances under which language-data is obtained in social-class comparisons, (although Labov ibid) did make an additional argument which will be further considered subsequently) arguments for the basic equality of language capabilities between social-classes have been based mainly on the concept of the equality of linguistic competence. However, the fact is that the acceptance of this concept as a valid reason for differing levels of linguistic capability does not eliminate the possibility that the linguistic performances required by opposed social class environments and situations might be so different that they result in different language behavior capabilities in lower and upper social class speakers. It seems to be the latter possibility that is suggested within the thesis of lower-social-class language disabilities; Bernstein (1972) if not before, states this very clearly.

In order to argue successfully against such a thesis, namely the contention that lower-social-class language systems are not sufficient, there would additionally need to be a valid demonstration that there is no difference in the kinds of language performances that are habitual at social-class extremes. If there are no habitual performance differences, then obviously the questions being discussed here would be fictitious ones created out of the misrepresentation of lower-social-class behaviour. If there are habitual performances, then this still would not in itself mean that the incidence of any specific abilities or disabilities is of an intellectual kind. And finally, even if it should be shown that some performance characteristics are indeed to be associated with specific intellectual abilities or disabilities, this would still be far removed from the position of Jensen (1969), Eynsenck (1971) and others against whom the LSA resolution on language equality (LSA Bulletin, March 1972) argued, since there would be no need assume an hereditary factor (or a racial factor) and to ignore, as Jensen and others do, the obvious sociological explanations that would be apparent for such abilities or disabilities. Apart, therefore, from the question of the equality of linguistic competence (which seems adequately answered in the Labov and LSA references already cited) there are two issues to be examined. One is whether specific intellectual abilities or disabilities do at all indicate specific intellectual abilities or disabilities; the other is whether habitual linguistic performances differ in different social-class environments, and if they do, in what ways and with what results.

The evidence so far presented that specific language characteristics indicate specific intellectual abilities or disabilities consists entirely of correlations between such language characteristics on the one hand and social class, measured intelligence and educational achievement on the other. Measured intelligence and educational achievement have long been shown to be determined by environment, and to be biased towards middle and upper-class norms because, inevitably, of the way in which the measuring instruments have to be (or have been) constructed and administered. Some of the relevant researches are Nisbet (1953), Ferguson (1954), Floud and Halsey (1957), Vernon (1955, 1965a and b, 1966, 1967), Bruner (et al. 1956, 1966), McClelland (et al. 1953, 1958, 1961), Douglas (1964), John (1962), Klein (1965), Goodnow (1968). It is therefore not surprising if the characteristics of low-social-class language correlate negatively with measured intelligence and educational achievement, while those of upper-social-class language do the opposite. Consequently, information about correlations between language characteristics and intelligence or achievement measurements cannot at this stage answer the question of whether specific language characteristics are responsible for specific abilities or disabilities. The nearest possible approach to an answer can come only from an examination of the language characteristics themselves that are in question, and an analysis of the cognitive tasks they actually permit speakers to perform or not to perform.

Essentially, in a very preliminary and anecdotal way, such an examination and analysis was attempted in Labov (1969), but the full range of language characteristics, their possible interrelationships and their total communication implications are yet to be studied. The specific language characteristics in question, cited as demonstrating social-class differences in language-related abilities, are as follows:

(a) Vocabulary as measured by the presence of higher-order lexical categories and proportions of types to tokens.

(b) Length of sentences or clauses or minimally terminable syntactic units (T units as in Loban [1963]).

(c) Complexity as measured by quantities of dependent clauses as a whole, or specific types of dependent clauses involving logical relationships.

(d) The occurrence of various phrase-types, including nominalizations or nominal groups that are in the nature of reduced-sentences.

(e) The frequency of use of adjectives, or adjective-type modification.

In Craig (1971a: 382–85), it was pointed out, that in terms of language characteristics such as these, Caribbean English-based Creole speech would have to be regarded as a Bernstein type of restricted code, but that at the same time Creole speakers who had begun to learn Standard English and to shift their speech progressively towards the Standard end of the continuum seemed, in terms of the same characteristics, to be acquiring an elaborated code. It was further pointed out that this phenomenon, in relation to codal differences, implied a contradiction in terms, since such differences should not be merely functions of different morpho-syntactic systems and be variable in the way they appear to be in the Creole/Standard English continuum. What seemed to be indicated here was that at the Creole or non-Standard end of the continuum there was a certain style of communication which produced the morpho-syntactic characteristics commonly taken as evidence of restricted coding, while at the Standard end of the continuum the communication style was different and resulted in the opposite characteristics. This difference in communication styles carried with it no evidence that the content of language, or the content that could possibly be treated in the two styles of language, was any different.

These indications were confirmed in a study of the use of language in young Jamaican children living in contrasting socio-economic environments (Craig 1971b), and some implications of this confirmation been discussed in Craig

(1972, 1973). In this work it was shown, by comparisons of the types of language characteristics set out in sets (a) to (e) one paragraph ago, and by comparison also of the total volume of language produced in a given time, that different communication styles were evident at opposite extremes of the continuum and that these styles had the following objective results, *given the same set of meanings at each end.*

At the Creole or non-Standard extreme: More basic sentence-forms and relationships, consequently shorter sentences, and also consequently more numerous sentences per given quantity of words. Concrete nominal and more direct verbal vocabulary. Fewer adjectives as a whole, but with verbs often doing the work of adjectives, since shorter and more numerous sentences permitted a relatively larger quantity of main verbs; for this same reason, less of some transformationally derived lexical subcategories and less diversity of vocabulary. A larger absolute quantity of words per unit of time, probably attributable to the fact that this communication style requires less complex internal organization before an output of language is made.

At the Standard extreme: Less basic and more transformationally derived sentence-forms and relationships, consequently longer sentences, and also consequently fewer sentences per given quantity of words. More vocabulary items that are non-concrete, generalized and transformationally derived. More adjectives as a whole, especially such adjectives as provide generalized labels for sets of behavioral characteristics that might otherwise be represented as strings of short verb-phrases; consequently greater diversity of vocabulary. A smaller absolute quantity of words per unit of time, probably attributable to the fact that this communication style requires a more complex internal organization before an output of language is made.

In effect, the characteristics of the two styles accrue from the cumulative results of Creole and Standard sentences like the respectively (a) and (b) examples which follow and, which are meaning equivalents in each case, though not morpho-syntactically alike.

1. (a) /im tel lai an tiif/
        him tell lie and him thief (i.e., "steals")
    (b) He is untrustworthy.
2. (a) / im laik waak bout an taak-taak wen im fi wok /
        him like walk about and talk-talk when him (ought) to work.
    (b) He likes to idle. Or: He is idlesome.

3. (a) / im na wier shuu, an im wok plenty moni /
       him not wear shoe, and him work plenty money.
   (b) He doesn't wear shoes although he earns much money.
4. (a) / im tek stuon hit the guot in a im ed, an di guot ded/
       him take stone hit the goat in him head, and the goat dead.
   (b) He killed the goat by hitting it in its head with a stone.

From contrasts like those in (1) and (2) will come short, "and" – linked sentences for the Creole or Non-standard speaker, while, for the Standard speaker, there will be none of these, but rather a single sentence with more generalized vocabulary items, most likely adjectives. From contrasts like those in (3), "and" – linked sentences with the appropriate intonation produced by the Creole or Non-Standard speaker, would be represented in the Standard speaker by main and subordinate clauses with logical connectors and a more abstract vocabulary. From contrasts like those in (4), the Standard speaker would obtain a single long sentence with transformationally derived phrases and vocabulary, while the non-Standard speaker will produce several short sentences, sometimes very loosely linked. But in each case, the underlying meanings being mediated in the two styles would be the same.

The preceding are merely a few examples, obviously not intended to be exhaustive; obviously too, there could be many other types of underlying meaning equivalences that could be differently represented in the two styles. It is also not the intention here to suggest that Creole or non-Standard speakers produce all their sentences in the relevant exampled style, and that Standard speakers always do correspondingly in their own characteristic style. The two suggested styles are envisaged as dominant characteristics at the respective social-class extremes, but it is to be expected that there will be times when there might well be no difference in styles over given stretches of actual speech at each social-class extreme. In the actual Jamaican study already referred to, where the differences between speakers are expressed in terms of the occurrence frequencies of linguistic items, these points emerge relatively clearly.

What has been suggested here is that the language characteristics often regarded as indicating intellectual abilities or disabilities in fact indicate nothing more than contrasting styles of communication. A common set of underlying meanings mediated in the two styles would have different surface-level results. These surface-level results are in the nature of habits that can be learned automatically as a natural part of the process of learning a Standard dialect; this explains why such learning not only results in a movement along the Creole or dialect continuum but appears also as a change from restricted to elaborated coding in terms of the characteristics so far suggested for these codes. There is no reason to suppose that the factors discussed here relevant to the Jamaican situation do not, at least in some measure, apply in other essentially bidialectal situations. The realities of dialect or quasi-dialect differences have generally been ignored in the whole theory of restricted and elaborated coding, even linguists who have always been aware of these realities have often erred by forgetting that the use of language always involves certain communication characteristics not so far described or describable in the orthodox formulations of phonology and grammar.

The question of the results of habit-formation through the constant use of a particular communication style, and constant involvement in a particular set of environmentally determined language-purposes and language-content characteristics, now deserves some attention.

It should not be surprising if speakers who are habituated in a particular communication style find it relatively more difficult to comprehend discourse in a style different from their own, even if phonology and grammar are held constant. When once the differently styled discourse is comprehended however, the relevant speakers would have no problem in reconstructing the discourse in their own particular style, even though they would be unable to reproduce it in the style in which they originally received it; that a capability similar to this exits in non-Standard speakers, and the implications of it, have been mentioned already as being illustrated in the work of Labov and Baratz earlier referred to in this section of the chapter. It is to be expected therefore that lower-social-class speakers would tend to find it relatively difficult to comprehend the dominant Standard-language communication style, while upper-social-class speakers would tend to find the opposite. It is also possible that lower-social-class speakers might acquire the phonology and grammar of Standard speech, while at the same time retaining the lower-social-class communication style and using it on most occasions, except when specially motivated to select the other style. This would explain the findings of later researchers in the Bernstein group that lower social-class children often have an elaborated code-available. The matter, however, probably goes further than this.

It is well known, from work such as that of Luria and Yodovich (1959), Luria (1961), and Vygotsky (1962), that the possession of appropriate language facilitates the performance of many types of cognitive tasks, of which many are ostensibly non-verbal; and it seems that many of the tasks required of school children are of the latter kind. Much more investigation needs to be done in this area, but it seems quite possible that the aspects of language that might be most facilitating in this way have to do with the availability of appropriate lexical labels for the specific percepts and relationships being dealt with, since the possession of an ability to use a label implies some prior mental acquaintance with, and orientation towards the relevant experience. It is consequently possible that the communication style and the language system linked to it at the Standard-language extreme might possess a larger repertoire of such facilitating lexical labels particularly in relation to cognitive tasks that are most relevant, in any case, to the upper-social-class subculture. If this is the case, then the habitual user of such a style might have some advantage over users of the opposite style in the performance of certain tasks required in conventional education, performance in intelligence and achievement tests, and so on.

At the same time, it is also quite possible that there are special characteristics of the Creole or non-Standard communication style and its own language system that might facilitate the performance of other kinds of tasks. It is possible, for example, that the dominance in this style of short, basic NP+VP combinations, very directly related to experience, might well be related to the superiority displayed in imaginative activity by the lower-social-status children studied by Geoffrey Turner (described in Bernstein 1972: 142); and there could possibly be other activities in which this particular communicative style might be more facilitating than the opposite style is.

The position taken here, and justified in the Jamaican study already cited, differs from that of Bernstein because the mentioned communication styles are regarded as contingent characteristics of respectively different morpho-syntactic systems, in such a way that the learning of one system confers the respective style, so long as that one system is being used without interference from the other. In this respect, the two types of communication are in a relation similar to that of two discrete natural languages; it might be easier to say certain things in one language than it is in the other, but the natural users of the two languages have the same cognitive and intellectual competence, and no one set of users possesses any absolute cognitive abilities or disabilities different from those of the other.

Apart from what has here been referred to as communication style and its usually contingent morpho-syntax, another aspect of language in which constant, socially determined habituation might possibly produce some cognitive result is the purposes, aims, and intentions with which language is used. It should not be surprising if social-class extremes differ in the detailed emphasis put upon such purposes, aims, and intentions; such differences, with reference to whole cultures and subcultures have been the burden of ethnographic studies from Malinowski (1923) to, for example, Hymes (1961a and b, 1962) and much of Gumperz and Hymes (1972). This aspect of the use of language would be reflected objectively in the narrow types of performative and illocutionary acts, in the sense of Austin (1962) and Searle (1969) that speakers are habituated to carry out in language; this aspect, it is important to note, could not possibly be revealed by the kinds of language characteristics (a to e earlier exampled) often examined in studies of social-class difference.

In the Jamaican study relevant here, it was found that lower-social-class children talking freely among themselves tended to engage in conversational exchanges involving questions, exclamations, commands, and various types of interpersonal adjustments more frequently than upper-social-class children did in similar circumstances. At first (e.g., Craig 1971b: 346–47) this indication seemed to agree with the Bernstein predication that children of this social class would be more strongly habituated than upper-social-class children towards communicating in shared referential situation, communicating for very prag-matic purposes, and so on. Subsequent consideration of the data has placed a reservation on this indication, which is that this trait of the children does not imply any "restriction" in the Bernstein sense, relative to their upper-social-class counterparts, but implies rather a relatively greater interest in their peers and in personal relationships. This conclusion seems supported by other evidence which will be mentioned subsequently.

The remaining aspects of language use in which specific constant habituation might have some determining effect on cognitive abilities may all be subsumed under the label: "content" of language; content in this sense refers to the objects, experiences and relationships that are treated in language. Differences in this aspect of language, if they exist, ought to be reflected objectively in the narrow semantic subclasses of grammatical categories and contextual assumptions that speakers are accustomed to communicate. In the study of Jamaican children here being referred to, lower-social-class children referred to persons, including adults, far more frequently than upper-social-class children did; this trait fitted well with the predominant interest of the former children, already referred to above, in interpersonal relationships. In traits such as egocentricity (commonly referred to in earlier codal studies) rural children showed the greater tendency and no appropriate absolute difference between upper and lower-social-class urban children was shown. Lower-social-class children showed a stronger tendency than upper-social-class children did to reference the present and immediate in both place and time. This is in accord with the prediction of the Bernstein theory, but here again a reservation (not as clearly evidenced in Craig

1971b, for example) has to be placed on the possible interpretation, since the children would in any case be obliged to make such references because of their already mentioned interests in their peers, in persons generally and in what usually happened immediately around them.

The parallel upper-social-class interest on the other hand, tended to be more anecdotal, referring more often to what happened once, as distinct from what usually happens. Lower-social-class children referred concepts of number, sequencing, and obligation (in modal verbs) more frequently than their upper-social-class counterparts did, but the latter referenced probability and possibility more frequently than the former. Causal, conditional, and concessive relationships did not discriminate strongly between the different sets of children, but upper-social-class boys made references to such concepts less than other children did. Altogether, these apparently habitual differences in the content of language seem strongly related to the dominant interests, types of relationships, and experiences that could naturally be expected in the contrasting social environments. There is no evidence that this kind of habituation in content would lead to any absolute cognitive abilities or disabilities.

The total evidence on social-class influences relevant to the language abilities of Jamaican children may be summarized as follows: most of the social-class language differences commonly referred to by previous researchers are differences in communication styles that have nothing to do with cognitive abilities, and that can be acquired with the learning of the specific morpho-syntactic systems to which they are related; differences in the purposes and content of language can inevitably be expected to appear and to differentiate between persons existing in different cultural environments, since the interrelationships between speakers, and the interests and life experiences of speakers can be expected to differ with environments. There is no evidence that habituation in specific styles, sets of language purposes and types of content create any absolute cognitive abilities or disabilities, but it does seem that many of the performances, including linguistic ones, required in conventional education are present more frequently, and can therefore be more easily learned, in upper-social-class than in lower-social-class environments. There are still some performances, however, that do seem to be facilitated by the lower-social-class experience. What most often happens in education is that the child of a lower-social class is often required to acquire certain learned responses which come naturally only in the upper-social-class environment; on the other hand no corresponding requirement is necessary that the upper-social-class child should acquire learned lower-social-class responses. The factors that have been considered here with special reference to the Jamaican situation seem to have relevance for all bidialectal or quasi-bidialectal situations in the English-official Caribbean as well as elsewhere.

One of the most important practical implications of the preceding is that the teaching of the Standard dialect also involves the teaching of a particular communication style. Some of the procedures that would need to be specially considered in such teaching are discussed in Craig (1972). The procedures involve taking what might otherwise be terminal Standard language strings, except for a lower-social-class communication style, and learning to proceed through the transformations that would transform such strings into the opposite communication style. For the non-Standard speaker learning the Standard, this type of learning might not be crucial from the point of view of language production, but it certainly seems to have an important bearing on the reception of Standard language. Without such learning, many originally non-Standard speakers who succeed in mastering the basic morphology and syntax of the Standard operate at a relatively low receptive level, a fact which seldom becomes evidenced until such speakers begin to experience the demands of higher education.

7. The Total Requirements of Education: A Summary

The increase, since the 1950s, of Creole language studies has brought with it an improved understanding of the sociolinguistic factors that operate in Creole or non-Standard dialect situations. In the Caribbean such situations are virtually bidialectal ones, as far as education is concerned, in the officially English-speaking territories. The situations bear some resemblance to the social-dialect or the lower-social-class ones in the United States of America and Britain, although social conditions and (especially in territories where there are strong survivals of basilect Creoles) linguistic ones too are often substantially different.

In the relevant territories, Standard English or a special variety of it is the language of education. However, although Creole or post-Creole speech is often regarded as closely identified with the national consciousness and identity, and is preserved for close personal exchanges and within the continued development of a vernacular culture, there does not seem to be any possibility, because of the dominant attitudes of the population, that such speech will be accepted as the official language or the language of education. In this context, schools are faced with the task of helping children to develop naturally and without inhibition in their home language, but at the same time to become fluent users of Standard speech.

Education authorities throughout the region recognize the need for a new approach to language education, so that the already stated task of schools might be achieved more efficiently than it has been in the past. However, especially in the context of economic underdevelopment and consequent scarcity of resources, educational innovations take a long time to reach the classroom; there are still classroom survivals of the procedure of teaching the Standard by correcting, and inhibiting the normal speech of children. Ideas of teaching the Standard by quasi-foreign language methods, have begun to make an impact , however, but even in the United States of America where such ideas have been most implemented, problems have been experienced and the returns of teaching are slow and small; similar problems are experienced in the English-official Caribbean, but the special procedures necessary for second-dialect teaching are being more carefully studied beginning with experiments in Jamaica; the results of the latter are being disseminated through other territories.

The total requirements of bidialectal education include much more than merely teaching the Standard dialect without inhibiting the child's home language. It includes a full utilization of the child's natural cultural environment, and at the same time it includes developing in the child the knowledge, skills, attitudes and cultural attributes necessary for mobility in the society as a whole. This total aim, when linked to the fundamental problem of language education, makes it imperative that the implications of relationships between language and other aspects of human behaviour be taken into consideration in educational planning. The most important factor in this connection is the relationship between language and social class, since the Creole or post-Creole speaker in the English-official Caribbean is characteristically an individual of low social class, while the Standard language and most of the aims and content of conventional education are indigenous to the upper social class. Studies of this relationship, again beginning in Jamaica, question the theory of lower-social-class deficiency, but suggest that the acquisition of Standard language involves more than the acquisition of phonology, morphology, and syntax; the results of this seem important for second-dialect teaching.

References

Aarons, B., and Stewart, W.A. (eds.) (1969), "Linguistic-cultural differences and American education", *The Florida FL Reporter*, Anthology issue.

Abrahams, R.D. (1970), "The advantages of black English", *Southern Conference of Language Learning,* Florida 1970.

Atlatis, J.W. (ed.) (1969), Twentieth Annual Round Table Meeting, Number 22. Georgetown University School of Linguistics.

Alleyne, M.C. (1961), "Communication and politics in Jamaica," *Caribbean Studies* 3.

———. (1963), "Language and society in St Lucia", *Caribbean Studies* 1 (1).

Allsopp, S.R.R. (1949–53), "The language we speak", *Kyk-over-all,* Vols. 2, 3, 5. Guyana.

———. (1958a), "The English Language in British Guiana", *English Language Teaching* 12 (2).

———. (1958b), "Pronominal forms in the dialect of English used in Georgetown (British Guiana) and its environs by people engaged in non-clerical occupations". MA thesis. University of London.

———. (1962), Expression of state and action in the dialect of English used in the Georgetown area of British Guiana". PhD dissertation. University of London.

———. (1965), British Honduras: The linguistic dilemma", *Caribbean Quarterly* 11 (3 and 4).

———. (1972a), "Some suprasegmental features of Caribbean English".

———. (1972b), "The problem of acceptability in Caribbean creolized English", in: *Creole Languages and Educational Development: Papers from the Conference Sponsored by UNESCO and UWI,* July 1972, ed. by D.R. Craig. To be published. London, New Beacon Publications.

Armstrong, B. (1968), "The teaching of English in Guiana", *The Guiana Teacher,* 2 (7).

Austin, J.L. (1962), *How To Do Things With Words,* ed. by J.O. Urmson. Harvard University Press.

Bailey, B.L. (1953), "Creole Languages of the Caribbean area." MA thesis. Columbia University.

———. (1962), *A Language Guide to Jamaica.* New York, Research Institute for the Study of Man.

———. (1963), "Teaching of English noun-verb concord in primary schools in Jamaica", *Caribbean Quarterly* 9 (4).

———. (1964), "Some problems in the language teaching situation in Jamaica", in: *Social Dialects and Language Learning,* by Roger W. Shuy. Champaign, Illinois, National Council of Teachers of English.

———. (1966), *Jamaican Creole Syntax: A Transformational Approach.* Cambridge University Press.

———. (1971), "Jamaican Creole: can dialect boundaries be defined?", in: Hymes (ed.).

Bailey, C.J. N. (1969–70), "Studies in three-dimensional language theory I–IV", *Working Papers in Linguistics.* University of Hawaii.

———. (1970), "Using data variation to confirm, rather than undermine, the validity of abstract syntactic structures", *Working Papers in Linguistics.* University of Hawaii.

Baratz, J.C. (1969), "*Teaching Black Children to Read.* Washington, DC, Center for Applied Linguistics.

Bennett, L. (1942), "Jamaica dialect verse: comp. George R. Bowen", *The Herald* Kingston.

———. (1943), *Jamaican Humour in Dialect.* Kingston, Gleaner Jamaica Press Association.

———. (1950), *Anancy Stories and Dialect Verse.* Kingston, Jamaica, Pioneer Press.

Bereiter et al. (1966), *Teaching Disadvantaged Children in the Preschool.* Englewood Cliffs, NJ,   Prentice-Hall Inc.

Bernstein, B. (1961A), "Social structure, language and learning", *Educational Research* 3.

———. (1961b), "Social class and linguistic developments: a theory of social learning", in: *Economy, Education and Society*, ed. by A.H. Halsey, J. Floud and A. Anderson. New York, The Free Press.

———. (1961c), "Aspects of language and learning in the genesis of the social process", *Journal of Child Psychology and Psychiatry* 1: 313. Reprinted, pp. 251–63 in: *Language, Culture and Society*, by D. Hymes.

———. (1962a), "Linguistic codes, hesitation phenomena are intelligence", *Language and Speech* 5: 31–46.

———. (1962b), Social class, linguistic codes and grammatical elements", *Language and Speech* 5: 221–24

———. (1965), "A socio-linguistic approach to social learning", in: *Social Science Survey*, ed. by J. Gould. London, Pelican.

———. (1966), "Elaborated and restricted codes: an outline", in: S. Lieberson (ed.).

———. (1972), "A critique of the concept of compensatory education", in: Cazden, John, and Hymes.

Berry, J. (1972), "Some observations on residual tone in West Indian English", in: Craig (ed.). To be published.

Bickerton, D. (1971), "Guyanese speech". Manuscript. University of Guyana.

———. (1971a), "Inherent variability and variable rules", *Foundations of Language* 7.

———. (1972), "The structure of polyectal grammars", in: Shuy (ed.), 1973.

———. (1973), "On the nature of a Creole continuum", *Language* 49 (3).

Brooks, C.K. (1964), "Some approaches to teaching English as a second language", in: Stewart (ed.).

Bronkhurst, H.V.P. (1888), *Among the Hindus and Creole of British Guiana.* London, T. Woolmar.

Bruner, J. et al. (1956), *A Study of Thinking.* London, Chapman & Hall.

———. (1966). *Studies in Cognitive Growth.* New York, Wiley.

Bull, W.E. (1955), "Review of: The use of vernacular languages in education", *IJAL 21*: 228–94.

Carrington, L.D. (1967), "St Lucia Creole: A descriptive analysis of its phonology and morphosyntax". PhD dissertation. Mona, University of the West Indies.

———. (1968), "English language learning problems in the Caribbean", *Trinidad and Tobago Modern Language Review* No. 1.

——. (1969), "Deviations from Standard English in the speech of primary school children in St Lucia and Dominica", *IRAL, Vol. VIII/3.*

——. (1970), "English language teaching in the Commonwealth Caribbean", *Commonwealth Education Liason Committee Newsletter* 2 (10).

Carrington, L.D., and Borely, C. (1969), "An investigation into English language learning and teaching problems in Trinidad and Tobago", Mimeographed, St Augustine, UWI Institute of Education.

Carrington, L.D., Borely, C., and Knight, E.H. (1972), *Away Robin Run: A Critical Description of the Teaching of the Language Arts in the Primary Schools of Trinidad and Tobago.* St Augustine, Trinidad and Tobago. St Augustine, Trinidad, Institute of Education.

Carroll, J.B. (1960), "Language development in children", in: Saporta (ed.), 1961.

Cassidy, F.G. (1961), *Jamaica Talk: Three Hundred Years of the English Language in Jamaica.* London, Macmillan.

Cassidy, F.G., and Le Page, R.B. (1967), *Dictionary of Jamaica English.* Cambridge University Press.

——. (1972), "Jamaican Creole and Twi: some comparisons", in: Craig (ed.), to be published.

Cave, G.N. (1970), "Sociolinguistic factors in Guyana language", *Language Learning* 20 (2).

——. (1971), *Primary School Language in Guyana,* Georgetown, Guyana Teachers' Association.

——. (1972), Measuring linguistic maturity: the case of the noun stream", in: Craig (ed.), to be published.

Cazden, C.B., John, V.P., and Hymes, D. (eds.) (1972), *Functions of Language in the Classroom.* New York, Columbia University, Teachers College Press.

Christie, P. (1969), "A sociolinguistic study of some Dominican Creole speakers". PhD dissertation. University of York.

Collymore, Frank (ed.) (1952 onwards), *Bim.* Barbados, Advocate Press.

Corbin, R., and Crosby, M. (1965), *Language Programs for the Disadvantaged.* Champaign, Illinois, NCTE.

Coulthard et al. (1968), "The structure of the nominal group and elaboratedness of code", *Language and Speech* 11 (2): 234–50.

Craig, D.R. (1964), "The written English of some 14-year-old Jamaican and English children" in: Faculty of Education. UWI.

——. (1966a), "Some developments in language teaching in the West Indies", *Caribbean Quarterly,* 12 (1).

——. (1966b), "Teaching English to Jamaican Creole speakers: A model of a multi-dialect situation", *Language Learning* 16 (1–2).

——. (1967), "Some early indications of learning a second dialect", *Language Learning* 17 (3and 4).

———. (1969), *An Experiment in Teaching English*. Caribbean University Press and London, Ginn and Co., Ltd.

———. (1971), "English in Secondary Education in a former British Colony: a case study of Guyana", *Caribbean Studies* 10 (4).

———. (1971a) "Education and Creole English in the West Indies: some sociolinguistic factors", in: Hymes (ed.), 1971.

———. (1971b), "The use of language by 7-year-old Jamaican children living in contrasting socio-economic environments". PhD thesis. University of London.

———. (1972), "Intralingual differences, communication and language theory", in: Craig (ed.), forthcoming.

———. (1973), "Social class, language and communication in Jamaican children", in: *Education in the Commonwealth* 6. London, Commonwealth Secretariat.

———. (Forthcoming) *Creole Languages and Educational Development: Papers from the Conference Sponsored by UNESCO and the UWI, July 1972*. London, New Beacon Publications.

Crow, L.D., et al. (1966), *Educating the Culturally Disadvantaged Child*. New York, David McKay Co.

Cruickshank, J.G. (1911), "Negro English with reference particularly to Barbados", *Timehri*, 3rd series, 1 (183).

———. (1916), *"Black talk". Being notes on negro dialect in British Guiana with (inevitably) a chapter on the vernacular of Barbados*. Guiana, The Agrosy Press.

Cuffie, D. (1964), "Problems in the teaching of English in the island of Trinidad from 1797 to the present day". MA thesis. University of London, Institute of Education.

DeCamp, D. (1971), "Toward a generative analysis of a post Creole speech continuum", in: Hymes (ed.), 1971.

———. (1972), "Standard English books and Creole speaking children", in: Craig (ed.), forthcoming.

Douglas, J.W.B. (1964), *The home the and school*. London and New York, MacGibbon and Kee.

Edwards, W. (1972), "'Have' and 'be' in Guyanese Creole", in: Craig (ed.), forthcoming.

Eysenck, H.J. (1971), *Race, Intelligence and Education*. London, Temple Smith.

Faculty of Education, University of the West Indies. 1965), "Language teaching, linguistics and the teaching of English in a multilingual society", *Report of the Conference at University of The West Indies*, April 1964.

Fasold, R.W. (1968), "Isn't English the first language too?", *NCTE Annual Conference, Wisconsin 1968*.

———. (1969), "Orthography in reading materials for black English speaking children", in: Baratz and Shuy (eds.), 1969.

Fasold, R.W. and Shuy, R.W. (eds.), (1970), "Teaching Standard English in the Inner City." Washington, DC, Center for Applied Linguistics.

Ferguson, G. (1954), "On learning and human ability", *Canadian Journal of Psychology* 8: 95–112.

Figueroa, J. (1962), "Language Teaching: Part of a general and professional problem", *English Language Teaching* 16 (3).

———. (1966), "Notes on the teaching of English in the West indies", *New World Quarterly* 2 (4).

———. (1972), "Some notes, together with samples of language occurring in the Creole context", in: Craig (ed.), forthcoming.

Fishman, J.A., and Leuders-Salmon, E. (1972), What has the sociology of language to say to the teacher? On teaching the standard variety to speakers of dialectal or societal varieties", in: Cazden, John, and Hymes (eds.), 1972.

Floud, J., and Halsey, A.H. (1957), Social class, intelligence tests and selection for secondary schools", in: Halsey, Floud, and Andefson (1961): 209–15.

Fries, C.C. (1922), *The Structure of English*. London, Longmans, Green, and Co.

———. (1940), "American English Grammar" *English Monograph* 10. Champaign, Illinois, NCTE.

Gaidoz, H. (1881), "Bibliographie Créole", *Revue Critique d'Histoire et de litérature* 13 (35 and 45).

Goodnow, J.J. (1968), "Cultural variations in cognitive skills", in: Prince-Williams (ed.), 1969.

Grant, D.R.B. (1964), "A study of some common language and spelling errors of elementary school children in Jamaica", in: Faculty of Education 1965.

Gray, C. (1963), "Teaching English in the West Indies", *Caribbean Quarterly* 9 (1–2).

Gumperz, J., and Hymes, D. (eds.), (1972), *Directions in Sociolinguistics: The Ethnography of Communication*. New York, Holt, Rinehart & Winston.

Hall, R.R. (1966), *Pidgin and Creole Languages*. Ithaca, NY, Cornell University Press.

Hawkins, R.R. (1969), "Social class, the nominal group and references", *Language and Speech*, 12, part 2: 125–35.

Hughes, A. (1966), " Non-Standard English of Grenada", *Caribbean Quarterly* 12 (4).

Hymes, D.H. (1961a), "Linguistic aspects of cross cultural personality study", in: *Studying Personality Cross Culturally*, ed. by Bert Kaplan. New York, Harper & Row.

———. (1961b), "Functions of speech: An evolutionary approach", pp. 55–83 in: *Anthropology and Education*, ed. by Fred Gruber, Philadelphia, University of Pennsylvania Press.

———. (1962), "The ethnography of speaking", in: *Anthropology and Human Behaviour*, ed. by T. Gladwin and W.C. Stuyvesant. Washington, DC, Anthropological Society of Washington.

Hymes, D.H. (ed.) (1971), *Pidginization and Creolization of Language*. Cambridge University Press.

Innis, L.O. (1910), *Trinidad and Trinidadians*. Trinidad, Mirror Printing Works.

———. (1923), *Creole Folklore and Popular Superstitions in Trinidad*. Trinidad, Yuilles Printerie.

Jensen, A.R. et al. (1969), *Environment, Heredity and Intelligence*. Harvard Reprint, Series No 2, 1969.

John, V.P. (1962), "The intellectual development of slum children", *American Orthopsy-chiatric Association Annual Meeting* 1962.

Jones, J.A. et al. (1966), "English in the West Indies", *English Language Teaching* 20 (2).

Kandel Subcommmittee (1946), *Report of the Secondary Education Continuation Committee*. Jamaica, Government Printery.

Klein, J. (1965), *Samples from English Cultures*. London, Routledge and Kegan Paul.

Knight, H.E., Carrington, L.D., and Borely, C.B. (1972), *Preliminary Comments on Language Arts Textbooks in Use in the Primary Schools of Trinidad and Tobago*. UWI, Institute of Education.

Kochman, T. (1969), "Social factors in the consideration of teaching Standard English", in Aarons and Stewart (eds.), 1969.

Labov, W. (1964), "Stages in the acquisition of Standard English", in: *Social Dialects and Language Learning*, ed. by Shuy. Champaign, Illinois, NCTE.

———. (1966), *The Social Stratification of English in New York City*. Washington DC, Center for Applied Linguistics.

———. (1969), *The Logic of Non-Standard English, Twentieth Annual Round Table Meeting*, No. 22, ed. by J.E. Alatis. Georgetown University School of Languages and Linguistics.

———. (1971), "The notion of 'system'", in: *Creole Languages*, ed. by Hymes.

Labov, W., and Cohen, P. (1967), "Systematic relation of Standard and non-Standard rules in the grammar of Negro speakers", *Project Literacy Report*, 8. Ithaca, New York, Cornell University.

Labov, W., et al. (1965), "A preliminary study if the structure of English used by Negro and Puerto Rican speakers in New York City", *Co-operative research Project* No. 3091, Mimeographed report. Columbia University.

Latrobe, C.J. (1837/38), Reports on Negro education, to Lord Glenelg, Secretary of State For Education and for War. Government of Great Britain.

Lawton, D.L. (1963), "Suprasegmental phenomena in Jamaica Creole". PhD dissertation. Michigan State University.

———. (1965), "Some problems of teaching a creolized language to Peace Corps Members", *Language Learning* 14.

———. (1971), "Tone and Jamaican Creole", Paper read at the Annual Conference on Caribbean Linguistics, May 17–21, Mona. Mimeo. UWI.

Lawton, D. (1963), "Social class differences in language development", *Language and Speech* 6 (3): 120–43.

———. (1964), "Social class language differences in group discussions", *Language and Speech* 7 (3): 182.

———. (1968), *Social Class, Language and Education*. London, Routledge and Kegan Paul.

Le Page, R.B. (1952), "A survey of dialects in the British Caribbean", *Caribbean Quarterly*, 2 (3).

———. (1955), "The Language problem in the British Caribbean", *Caribbean Quarterly* 4 (1).

———. (1957), "General Outlines of English Creole Dialects", *Orbis* 6.

Le Page, R.B. (ed.) (1961), *Proceedings of the Conference on Creole Language Studies, 1961*. London, Macmillan.

———. (1972), "The concept of competence in a Creole English situation", in Craig, (ed.), forthcoming.

Le Page, R., and DeCamp, D. (1960), *Jamaican Creole: An Historical Introduction to Jamaican Creole by R.B. Le Page and Four Jamaican Creole Texts, by David DeCamp*. London, Macmillan.

Lieberson, S. (ed.) (1966), "Explorations in sociolinguistics", *Social Enquiry* 36.

LSA Bulletin (1972), *Linguistic Society of America Bulletin*, March.

Loban, W. (1963), "The language of elementary school children", NCTE, Research Report No. 1.

Long, Edward (1774), *The History of Jamaica*. Great Britain.

Luria, A.R., and Yudovich, I. (1959), *Speech and the Development of Mental Processes in the Child*. London, Staples Press.

Luria, A.R. (1961), *The Role of Speech in the Regulation of Normal and Abnormal Behaviour*. London and New York, Pergamon Press.

McClelland, C.L. et al. (1953), *The Achievement Motive*. New York, Appleton-Century-Crofts.

———. (1958), *Talent and Society: New Perspectives in the Identification of Talent*. Princeton, New Jersery, Van Nostrand.

Malinowsky, B. (1923), "The problem of meaning in primitive cultures", in: *The Meaning of Meaning*, by C.K. Ogden and I.A. Richards. London, Routledge and Kegan Paul.

Nisbet, J. (1953), "Family environment and intelligence", in: Halsey, Floud, and Anderson (1961): 273–87.

Norwood Committee (1943), *Curriculum and Examinations in Secondary Schools*. HMSO.

Reissman, F. (1962), *The Culturally Deprived Child*. New York, Harper and Row.

Reissman, Karl (1961), "The English-based Creole of Antigua", (Research Notes), *Caribbean Quarterly* 1 (1).

———. (1965), "The isle is full of noises: A study of Creole in the speech pattern of Antigua, West Indies". PhD dissertation. Harvard University.

Rice, F.A. (ed.) (1962), *Study of the Role of Second Languages in Asia, Africa, and Latin America*. Washington, DC, Center for Applied Linguistics.

Robinson, W.P. (1965), "The elaborated code in working class language", *Language and Speech* 8, part 4, Oct.–Dec., 1965: 243–52.

Robinson, W.P., and Creed, C.D. (1968), "Perceptual and verbal discriminations of 'elaborated' and 'restricted' code users", *Language and Speech* 11 (3): 182–93.

Russell, T. (1868), *The Etymology of Jamaica Grammar* by a Young Gentleman. Kingston, MacDougall & Co.

Saporta, Sol, (ed.) (1961), *Psycholinguistics*. New York, Holt, Rinehart & Winston.

Schaedel, R. (ed.) (1969), *Research and Resources of Haiti*. New York, Research Institute for the Study of Man.

Schuchart, H. (1882), *Kreolish Studein*, 11 vols. Vienna.

Scoles, I. (1885), *Sketches of African and Indian Life in British Guiana*. Guiana, The Argosy Press.

Searle, J.B. (1969), *Speech Acts: An Essay in the Philosophy of Language*. Cambridge University Press.

Shuy, R.W. (1972), "Strategies for implementing sociolinguistic principles in the schools", in: Craig (ed.), forthcoming.

Shuy, R.W. (ed.) (1964), *Social Dialects and Language Learning*. Champaign, Illinois, NCTE.

———. (1972), Proceedings of the 23rd Annual Round Table. Washington DC, Georgetown University.

Shuy, R.W., Wolfram, W.A., and Riley, W.K. (1967), "Linguistic correlates of social stratification", in: *Detroit Speech*, Final Report. Co-operative Research Project 6-1347. Office of Education.

Solomon, D. (1966), "The system of predication in the speech of Trinidad: a quantitative study of decreolization". MA thesis. Columbia University.

———. (1972), "Form, content and the post-Creole continuum", in: Craig (ed.). 1974.

Spears, R. (1972), "Pitch and intonation in Cayman English", in: Craig (ed.), forthcoming.

Stewart, W.A. (ed.) (1962), "Creole languages in the Caribbean", in: Rice (ed., 1962).

———. (1967), "Sociolinguistic factors in the history of American negro dialects", *The Florida FL Reporter* 5 (2).

———. (1969), "Negro dialect in the teaching of reading", in: Baratz and Shuy (eds.), 1969.

Stewart, W.A. (ed.) (1964). *Non-Standard Speech and the Teaching of English*. Washington, DC, Center for Applied Linguistics.

Taylor, D. (1945), "Certain Carib morphological influences on Creole", *International Journal of American Linguistics* 11 (3).

———. (1952), "A note on the phoneme /r/ in Dominican Creole", *Word* 8 (3).

———. (1955), "Phonic interference in Dominican Creole", *Word* 11.

———. (1961), "Some Dominican Creole descendants of the French definite article", in: *Conference on Creole Language Studies*, ed. by Le Page. London, Macmillan.

———. (1963), "Remarks on the lexiçon of Dominican French Creole", *Romance Philology* 16.

———. (1968), "New languages for old in the West indies", in: *Readings in the Sociology of Language*, ed. by J.A. Fishman. The Hague, Mouton.

Thomas, J.J. (1869), *The Theory and Practice of Creole Grammar*. (Reprinted London, New Beacon Books, 1969).

Trotman, J. (1973), "The teaching of English in Guyana: A linguistic approach". Mimeo. Faculty of Education, University of Guyana.

Tyndall, B. (1965), "Some grammatical aspects of the written work of Creolese-speaking school children in British Guiana". MA thesis. University of Manchester.

———. (1973), "Reading habit and the written expression of secondary school first formers". Mimeo. Faculty of Education, University of Guyana.

UNESCO (1953), "The use of vernacular languages in education: monographs on fundamental education". Paris.

Valdman, A. (1969), "The language situation in Haiti", In: Schaedel (ed.), 1969.

van Name, A. (1870), "Contributions to Creole grammar", *Transactions of the American Philological Association*, 1. Boston.

van Sertima, J. (1897), "Among the common people of British Guiana", *British Guiana Pamphlet*, No. 35.

———. (1905), *The Creole Tongues of British Guiana*. Berbice, British Guiana, The British Gazette Store.

Vernon, P.E. (1955), "The bearing of recent advances in psychology on educational problems", *Studies in Education* 7. University of London, Institute of Education.

———. (1965a), "Environmental handicaps and intellectual development", *British Journal of Educational Psychology*, 35: 1–12; 117–26.

———. (1965b), "Ability factors and environmental influences", *American Psychologist* 20: 723–33.

———. (1966), "Education and Intellectual development among Canadian Indians and Eskimos", *Educational Review* 18: 79–91; 186–95.

———. (1967), "Abilities and educational attainments in an East African environment", in: Price-Williams (ed.).

Walters, E. (1958), "Learning to read in Jamaica". Mona, Jamaica, UWI, Department of Education.

Warner, M. (1967), "Language in Trinidad with special reference to English". MA thesis, University of York.

Westmaas, D.A. (1948), "On writing Creolese" *Kyk-Over-All*, 2 (7), Guyana. "Some more aspects of Creolese". *Kyk-Over-All*, 5 Guyana.

Wilson, E. (1968), "Grammar in English teaching", *The Guiana Teacher*, 2 (7).

Winford, D. (1972), "A sociolinguistic description of two communities in Trinidad". PhD thesis. University of York.

Wolfram, W. (1969), *A sociolinguistic Description of Detroit Negro Speech*. Washington, DC, Center for Applied Linguistics.

———. (1970), "Sociolinguistic alternatives in teaching reading to non-standard speakers", *Research Quarterly* 4 (1). Delaware.

3 | Reading and the Creole Speaker

By 'Creole' is meant the kind of speech usually referred to as the 'dialect' in Jamaica. It is well known that the sounds, and syntax of this kind of speech differ from those of English. What we wish to discuss here, very briefly, is how these differences are likely to affect the Creole speaker who is learning to read.

The main problem for the Creole speaker, irrespective of his age or her age, is that teachers of reading often require speakers to do two complex things simultaneously. These two things are (1) to learn the relationship between written or printed shapes and the meanings they represent; and (2) to perceive or vocalize the latter meanings in terms of English sounds, English word forms and English syntax.

For the Creole speaker learning to read, both of these things are new and have to be learned. For the English speaker, however, only (1) has to be learned since (2) is automatic. The problems of the Creole speaker learning to read are therefore likely to be far greater than those of a normal English speaker in the same position.

Some teachers might wish to argue that most Jamaican Creole speakers have some passive knowledge of English and that just as these speakers, when they hear English speech, can understand some amount of it and infer the meaning of the rest, in the same way these speakers can directly understand a good deal of written or printed English and can infer the meaning of the rest from the general context.

But this argument cannot really stand. In listening to English speech, the Creole speaker can and does recognize and interpret the main English words which tend to be similar to those in Creole speech, and it is easy for him or her, when listening, to concentrate on those sounds that are easily recognizable and to ignore all the other sounds; in this way the Creole speaker can indeed get some meaning out of listening to English. But the Creole speaker learning to read cannot do the equivalent to this in reading; no person at all can be expected to do this at the beginner stage in reading; only a very skilful and mature reader knows how to get meaning out of reading-material by skimming over it and picking out the essential vocabulary items.

We may at this point briefly examine some details of the difficulty faced by the Creole speaker who is required to do (2) above, i.e., to perceive and vocalize written or printed meanings in terms of English sounds, word-forms and syntax. We may begin with sounds.

The main ways in which the sounds of Creole speech can sometimes differ from those of some kinds of English are illustrated by the following examples which are not meant to be exhaustive.

3.	English Sound	Examples of Words as Spelled	Creole Sound and Word Pronunciation

(Note: 'ʊ' is the sound heard in English 'full'; 'ʌ' is heard in English 'bus': the other sounds can be easily perceived from the word-examples given.)

English Sound	Examples of Words as Spelled	Creole Sound and Word Pronunciation
th [θ]	thin, thick	t: tin, tik [t]
dh[ð]	this, that	d: dis, dat [d]
er [ə]	thinner, thicker	a (1) : tina, tika [a]
zh [ž]	measure, treasure	j: meja, teeja [ž]
o (1) [ɒ]	hot, spot, rot	a (2): (h)at, spat, rat [a]
o (2) [ɔɔ]	off, yawn	aa: aaf, yaan [a:]
v [v]	river, never	b: riba, neba (now becoming rare) [b]
t (medially)[t]	little, bottle	k: likl, bokl [k]
k (initially) [k]	cat, car	ky: kyat, kyar [ky]
g initially) [g]	girl, garden	gy: gyal, gyaadn [gy]
b (initially) [b]	boy	bw: bwai [bw]

h (initially) [h]	him, house	im, ous Ø
w (initially) [w]	woman, would-:	-: uman, ud Ø
st (initially) [st]	stand-up, story	t: tanop, tuori [t, tw]
ng (finally) [ŋ]	singing, killing	n: singin, kilin [n]
nd (finally) [nd]	sand, hand	n: san, (h)an [n]
rst (finally) [rst]	first, burst	s: fos, bos [ɒ]
st (finally) [st]	test, rust	s: tes, ros Ø
rn (finally) [rn]	burn, turn	n: bon, ton [n]
sk (finally) [sk]	ask, husk	ks: aks, (h)oks [ks]
ilm (finally) [ɪ/]	film	lim: flim [lɪm]
rd, rt, rk		
(finally) [rd, rt, rk]	garden, heart, mark	d, t, k: gyaadn, haat, maak [ya:], [a]
initial and [ɑ]	afraid, because,	-fried, kaaz
medial [b]	ashamed, somebody,	-shiem, smadi Ø
syllables [ər]	yesterday, government	-yeside, govment [ɪde], [Ø]

In reading, a Creole speaker can, and often does, vocalize English spellings, such as those illustrated above, in terms of the Creole system of sounds, i.e., the Creole speaker would naturally tend to use a Creole pronunciation for the words that are being read. But in many cases, the Creole speaker, who is learning to read, is not allowed to use a Creole pronunciation freely, and is expected, instead, to produce English sounds, which he or she is unaccustomed to produce. In such cases, the teacher's insistence on a non-Creole pronunciation can inhibit the reader and increase the difficulty experienced by the latter in learning to associate visual shapes with meanings.

How many teachers, for example, would permit the pupil, without correction, to say uman for 'woman' or bokl for 'bottle' or smadi for 'somebody', while the pupil is reading? It is true that, in cases like these, the normal spelling of words is much closer to the English than to the Creole pronunciation, and that a phonic approach to reading would give the Creole speaker a good idea of the appropriate English sounds; but the difficulty of approaching meanings indirectly through a system of relatively strange sounds would still remain. The result is likely to be 'word-calling' rather than reading.

It is worthwhile to consider that the aim of teaching English pronunciation is one which can best be pursued in many ways separate and apart from the aim of teaching reading. It is possible that pursued in such ways, the pupil's learning of English pronunciation (if this is considered an acceptable goal) might become firmly based and evidenced in his or her reading; but it is unreasonable to expect reading and new pronunciation to be effectively and easily acquired by means of one and the same kind of activity. There are many detailed aspects of this question which cannot be dealt with here, but the nature of the problem ought to be clear.

The problem faced by the Creole speaker in attempting to vocalize and interpret English sounds while reading is accompanied by an even more serious problem involving the forms of words and the grammatical relationships between words in the material being read. The reason for this is that the ability to read fluently and with understanding greatly depends upon the reader being constantly able to perceive many different types of word-form and grammatical clues which tell him or her what to expect in the reading material that the eye has not yet reached. In addition, the reader often has to rely on such clues in order to make full sense out of material that the eye has already passed over.

This reliance on word-form and grammatical clues does not involve any conscious knowledge of grammar on the part of the reader. The relevant knowledge is unconscious and is naturally acquired by speakers by the time they reach age 5–6 years. It is the kind of 'automatic' knowledge which enables the child of that age to operate whatever are the basic grammatical rules that belong to the language of his or her environment. In this respect, Creole has its own grammatical rules and English has its own and a different set.

Below are some examples of how English word-form and grammatical clues assist the English-speaking, but not the Creole-speaking reader.

Firstly, because English uses certain inflections and other grammatical markers which are meaningful in English, but which Creole does not use, some of the earlier parts of sentences give to the English-speaking, but not to the Creole-speaking reader, indications of what to expect in later parts. Because of this the English-speaking reader does not need to spend as much time as the Creole-speaking reader does on the distinct phonic recognition of all sentence elements.

The following are some examples of this:

(i)   Singular or plural or compounded subjects (e.g. man, men, the man and the boy) tell the English-speaking but not the Creole-speaking reader whether to expect *is/are, was/were, has/have,* and verb-forms like *eat/*

eats, and so on, in the later parts of some sentences. (For pairs of items such as the latter, Creole tends to have only a single invariable form in each case).

(ii) Time and aspectual adverbs like *yesterday, two hours ago, usually*, and so on, in the earlier parts of sentences tell the English-speaking, but not the Creole-speaking reader that verb-forms marked to show certain specific tenses are sure to follow. The English-speaking, but not the Creole-speaking, reader will thereafter tend automatically to recognize and produce these tense-forms without needing to isolate the relevant individual phonic constituents of words.

Secondly, inflected and otherwise marked forms such as those just mentioned, together with the English inflected pronoun system *(who/whom/whose, he/him/his, she/her/hers, they/them/theirs*, and so on, not found in Creole) make it relatively easier for the English-speaking than for the Creole-speaking reader to identify cross-references and inter-relationships between themes and topics in the material being read. The latter kind of identification becomes particularly important in reading which involves no contextual clues other than those inherent in the words on the page.

Thirdly, where the English-speaking reader has no vocabulary problem, the Creole-speaking reader can possibly have one even though the essential meanings in the reading material are well within the experiences of both. The word 'few' on the reading page, for example, might not prove immediately accessible to a person who is accustomed to representing the same idea as 'one-one' *(wan-wan)*, and an adjective phrase such as: 'with touches of red here and there' could be an elaborate piece of nonsense to a person who would normally say *redi-redi* to express the same idea.

Fourthly, some forms of the English sentence taken as wholes can be an obstacle to quick understanding on the part of the Creole-speaking reader. This is probably so for the following reasons:

(i) Creole regularly has a "zero-copula" sentence, e.g., 'the book red,' 'the boy frighten,' and so on where English would use a copula: e.g., 'the book is red', the boy was frightened', and so on.

(ii) The English sentence-form beginning: There is/ are does not exist in Creole.

(iii) The very prevalent Creole sentence form that begins with the Creole particle a e.g., *a dat mi waan* ("That is what I want"), *a sik im sik* ("What is wrong with him is that he is sick" (one possible meaning)), does not exist in English and has no simple English sentence-form equivalent. English tends to express the equivalent meanings in ways that are generally unfamiliar to the Creole speaker.

There are possibly other ways additional to those so far mentioned in which English word-forms and grammar could result in reading problems for the habitual Creole speaker, but the preceding seem sufficient as examples. The question that now suggests itself is: what strategies might best be adopted in reading instruction to take the Creole language situation into account? This is the kind of question that has already been asked in some similar language situations in other parts of the world and the answers are new.

One answer might be to produce Creole-language materials for initial and early reading so that the Creole speaker might learn to read in the familiar language of his immediate environment, after learning to read; the Creole speaker would then be able to transfer his specific reading skills to the reading of English materials. However, for many reasons which we need not to go into here, this is not likely to be accepted in Jamaica as a possible solution to the problem, in just the same way as this solution, after some trial, recently proved unworkable in the USA. dialect situation.

There are two other possible answers, however, which can only be mentioned here, but which it is possible for teachers to explore further. The first of these is that it may be possible for the language of initial reading materials to be controlled in such a way that only such English word-forms and grammar as are already present in Creole speech would appear in the materials. For example, initial reading materials might contain sentences like these:

(A) Come Joe
     Sit down with Bibs and Sis
     See what we have
     A big, ripe mango.

but they would not contain sentences like these:

(B) Bibs and Sis *are sitting* down
     Sis *has* a mango
     Joe goes and *sits* with Bibs and Sis

because word-forms and grammar such as those underlined in (B) are not naturally found in Creole speech. The Creole speaker would find it easier to learn the initial reading skills from material such as exampled in (A) where the language problem is *avoided*. After the Creole speaker has learned the initial reading skills by using such reading material, he or she would find it easier to apply these skills to other material where the language is strange and unfamiliar.

The second other possible answer is for reading and the basic structures of English to be taught concurrently so that the Creole speaker is enabled to become familiar with the use of the language that he is learning to read. This would require that a programme of structural language practice (and note: this is not the same thing as memorizing grammatical rules) be carried out simultaneously and in close integration with the reading programme.

For Further Reading

Baratz, Joan C. and Roger W. Shuy, (eds). 1969. *Teaching Black Children to Read*. Washington DC: Center for Applied Linguistics.

Bailey, Beryl. 1966. *Jamaican Creole Syntax*. Cambridge: Cambridge University Press.

International Reading Association. 1970–. *Reading Research Quarterly* 6 and subsequent volumes.

4 | The Sociology of Language Learning and Teaching in a Creole Situation

1. Relevant Characteristics of Creole Speech Communities

A Creole language is one that has come into existence, no matter by which of several possible processes, as a result of the contact of speakers of different languages. In defining a Creole language in this way, however, we need to exclude from consideration such languages as some of the standard European languages, which started off in the same way as Creole languages but which, through centuries of national development, have achieved the status of standard national languages. Creole languages, therefore, recognized in this way, tend to be relatively new languages, spoken habitually mainly by persons who happen to be natives of newly-developing socio-economic communities; and in such communities there is usually some older, socio-politically dominant and more prestigious language that has originally been, or has become, the official language of the territorial area. A Creole language therefore tends to be of low social prestige, or to have a recently past history of being so, with persons who possess it as their only language being correspondingly low in the social hierarchy.

Based on the relationship between a Creole language and the more extensively-accepted standard language that exists in the same territorial area, two types of Creole language situations may be distinguished. In the first type, the Creole language is lexically, and perhaps grammatically as well, related to the more-extensively-accepted standard language. In the second type of situation there is no lexical or grammatical relationship, except perhaps for sporadic borrowings, between the Creole and the relevant standard language.

Some countries that provide examples of the first type of situation are Haiti and the French Caribbean, where the official language is French and the Creole is French-based; Sierra Leone, New Guinea and the officially English-speaking Caribbean where the former official language has been English and the Creoles have English as one of their bases. Some examples of the second type of situation are Surinam (Dutch Guiana) where the official language has been English and the Creoles have English as one of their bases. Some examples of the second type of situation are Surinam (Dutch Guiana) where the official language is Dutch and Creole such as Saramaccan and Sraanan are English/African-based; St Lucia (English-official Caribbean) and the Seychelles, where the official language is English and the Creoles are French-based. The vast majority of Creole-language areas (cf. Hancock 1971) seem to be of the first type (Craig 1977).

2. Creole-Standard Bilingualism

From what has so far been outlined it is clear that Creole speech communities will tend towards being bilingual communities. In such communities, whether a speaker naturally acquires the Creole language alone, or the more-extensively-accepted standard language alone, or both of the latter forms of language, will depend on the pattern of social stratification in the community and the position of the particular speaker within that pattern. The situation may be roughly described as diagrammed in Figure 4.1.

As a general rule, the lower the socioeconomic status of the individual, the more likely he or she is to be a monolingual Creole speaker; conversely, the higher the socioeconomic status, the more likely is it that the individual will acquire the more-extensively-accepted standard. Within this general rule, whether there will be individuals who naturally acquire both the Creole and the more-extensively-accepted standard will depend on factors such as the nature and extent of the interaction between social class, and the motivations that are generated within the community to use each form of language in different functional roles.

In general, the more-extensively-accepted standard language will tend to function as the medium of the official and formal business of the community, the

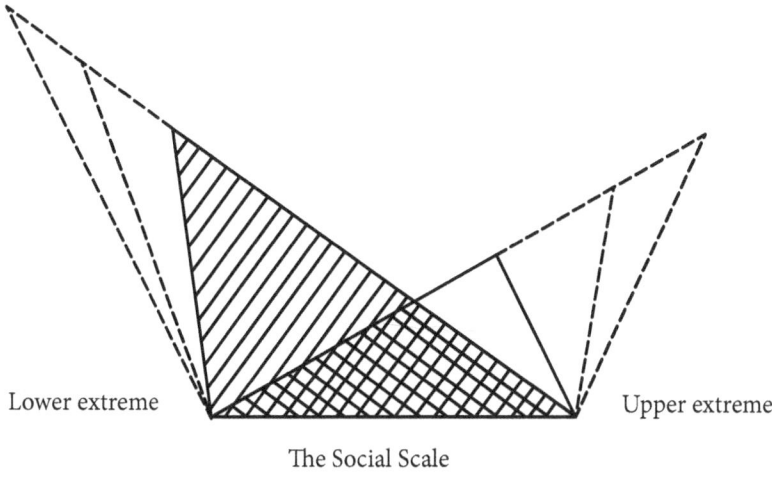

Lower extreme   Upper extreme

The Social Scale

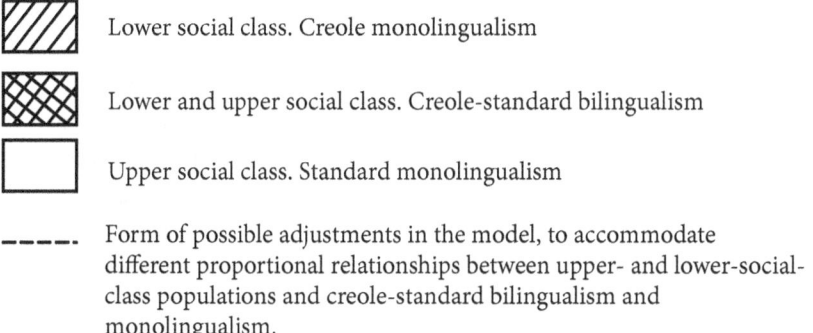

Lower social class. Creole monolingualism

Lower and upper social class. Creole-standard bilingualism

Upper social class. Standard monolingualism

_ _ _ _ .   Form of possible adjustments in the model, to accommodate
different proportional relationships between upper- and lower-social-
class populations and creole-standard bilingualism and
monolingualism.

Figure 4.1. Social class and language in a Creole language community

indicator of social distance, education, high status and importance; the Creole
language, on the other hand, will tend to be the language of informality and
intimacy, and of identification with the uniquely indigenous cultural tradition.

The development of Creole-Standard bilingual proficiency is, however, not
likely to be equally distributed between social-class extremes. Most often, it
seems to be the Creole language that is more widely diffused across the community, while the more-extensively-accepted standard tends to remain the
preserve of the upper social class and those who attain such status through
education. This happens because of the numerical superiority of the lower
social classes, and the fact that the dominant direction of social mobility is
from lower to upper with the result that lower-social-class individuals moving
to a higher status, with or without achieving a command of standard language,
take their Creole language with them; in addition to this, the proportion of the

upper-social, standard-speaking class which tends to achieve a proficiency in Creole through childhood contact with Creole-speaking children and providers of services and by other means will be larger than the comparable proportion of lower-social, Creole speakers who achieve standard language proficiency. These proportional relationships can be adequately represented in a model of the kind constructed at Figure 4.1.

The generalizations so far suggested in discussion and in the model seem valid for Creole-Standard speech communities as far removed and different as those of Jamaica (cf Le Page and DeCamp 1960; Cassidy 1961; Bailey 1966), Haiti (cf. Valdman 1969), urban Nigeria (cf. Adekunle 1972; Vincent 1972) and Papua New Guinea (cf. Sankoff and Laberge 1974; Wurm 1977), to mention just a few.

The tendencies of Creole-Standard bilingualism outlined above account, by implication, for what can be expected to happen when a Creole language becomes accepted in its territory as the Standard language or a Standard language, as has happened contemporaneously in Papua New Guinea, for example. The Creole takes on additional functions as a medium of the official and formal business of the community; this occurrence, however, is likely to be accompanied by significant attitudinal changes and conflicts in the language community as a whole. Some proficient users of the Standard will see the new status of Creole as representing a decline in the cultural values that are associated with education and refined literacy; others will see it as signifying the emergence of a more egalitarian type of society and the end of the socioeconomic and political discrimination which has language as one of its bases. No matter how it is viewed, however, the achieving of standard language status by a Creole will be accompanied, if not preceded, by a strengthening of its role as a preserver of the indigenous culture, including the folk tradition in song, narrative and humour; and there will tend to be an increase in its use for communicating these aspects of culture in advertising and other uses of the popular media.

It may be noted however, that even in some places, where, unlike Papua New Guinea, the Creole has been accorded no official status, as in the English-official Caribbean, the achieving of political independence by indigenous communities has often led to a similar intensification of the indigenous culture-preserving and culture-communicating role of the Creole.

Whether or not a Creole language is accorded an official status in its territory, however, it seems unlikely that a Creole-speaking community will ever be able to move, under present-day conditions, to a position of completely abandoning the older and more-extensively-accepted standard language that originally served as the official language. The reason for this is the advantage to the community of possessing a national language which is at the same time international in its acceptability.

3. Social Awareness, Creole and Standard Language

From what has already been said, it is not surprising to find that speakers in Creole-Standard speech communities, if they achieve a bilingual competence, tend to switch from one language to the other, often in the process of a single discourse, according to the varied social factors and personal interrelationships that impinge upon the discourse. Thus, a conversation between friends that began spontaneously in Creole might change, equally spontaneously, to standard language because a stranger of some importance has joined the group; or an indigenous speaker to a largely indigenous group on a public occasion might begin in standard language and either switch occasionally into Creole, deliberately in order to gain desired effects, or might lapse into Creole without being aware of it if he or she gets carried away by the heat of the discourse. Occurrences of the latter types have long been reported for English-based Caribbean and some other Creoles (Craig 1966; Bickerton 1971, 1973; Valman 1969).

Much of the code-switching and 'diglossia' (Ferguson 1959) that has been reported in Creole-Standard situations, however, involves, not a clear movement from one type of language to the other, but a complex blending or mixing of the two forms of language. In some Creole-speech situations, like that of Haiti (cf. Valdman 1969), this blending of Creole and standard, if it occurs at all, seems to be purely idiosyncratic and is not known to result in a discretely describable form of language that can be said to have a population of speakers. In some other Creole-speech situations, however, notably in the officially English-speaking Caribbean, apart from the mixing of Creole and Standard items that occurs in code-switching and diglossia, there is a fossilized blend of Creole and Standard features that constitutes the sole language of some speakers and that has become known as the 'mesolect' (cf. Bickerton 1973; Rickford 1974; Craig 1978a).

The phenomenon of mesolectal language is quite complex. Undoubtedly it represents the fossilization of an interlanguage, to use the terms of Selinker 1972 which are now well known. But why a mesolect should develop between Creole (basilect) and Standard (acrolect) (cf. Stewart 1962) in the territories of the English-based Caribbean Creoles, but not similarly develop, as has been reported, in the territories of the French-based Creoles has not yet been clearly accounted for. If the reports are correct, then the explanation probably rests in the differences between patterns of social mobility in the former British territories and those in the French territories. It would appear, that in the British territories, the motivation of the lower social classes towards upward social mobility was strong enough and elementary educational opportunities sufficiently available for there to be a constant striving towards the acquisition of Standard English, since the latter was the most immediately apparent passport to higher social status (cf. Bailey 1964) relevant to Jamaica; the result of such striving was, in many cases, an interlanguage between Creole and Standard. The persistence of this interlanguage, with all the attendant implications that are now understood relevant to interlanguages (cf. Selinker 1972; Richards 1972; Schumann 1974; Craig 1978a) is responsible for the range of language variation, that is known as the Caribbean Creole-language continuum (cf. DeCamp 1971; Bickerton 1973).

In summary, it may be said that the awareness of social stratification, of its implications, and of its correlation with the possession of Creole or Standard language provides, in Creole-language communities, a constantly strong motivation, not always successfully realized, towards the acquisition of a bilingual proficiency. Most often, the striving towards bilingualism is by Creole speakers aspiring to possess the standard; but if the community develops recognizable function roles for a Creole language, like, for example: its use by Ghanaian youths as in-group language (cf. Ansre 1978), its use in Haiti as the language of adult literacy (cf. Pompilus 1973), and so on, then the striving towards bilingualism might also proceed from standard-language speakers wishing to be proficient in Creole.

4. Language Learning and Teaching

The natural acquisition and informal learning of language in Creole situations is determined by the factors which have just been outlined in the preceding sections of this paper: the correlation between social class and type of language, the effects of social awareness and of possibilities of social mobility, the allocation by the community of different functional roles to different types of language, and the language attitudes that provide a basis for that allocation. Any formal attempt to teach language in such situations must therefore take cognizance of the latter factors and of the ways in which they can affect (a) the choice of language-education alternatives for the community as a whole, and

(b) the educational strategies and material that should be used in implementing any chosen alternative.

Decisions in relation to (a) and (b) preceding will involve language planning and will determine the conditions to be observed in the use of language in education at all levels. However, for most Creole situations, the most crucial level for the implementation of such decisions is that of primary education, since whatever is decided upon at this level, in terms of planning for the community as a whole, will become the basis of continuing strategies for other levels. The issues that are relevant to language learning and teaching in primary education in Creole situations have been discussed at some length in Craig 1977 and can be no more than merely referred to here.

First of all, the conditions that govern Creole-Standard bilingualism and that have been discussed in Section Two of this paper necessitate that, for any Creole speech community, alternatives in bilingual education such as those discussed, for example, in Fishman and Lovas 1970 be considered relative to Creole and Standard language. The decisions involved concern the following:

> 2(i) whether the Creole will be used in early education to the extent necessary to allow children to adjust to formal schooling and to learn sufficient of the community's standard language for it to become the medium of instruction (Transitional Bilingualism), (ii) whether both Creole and standard are to be developed in school for aural-oral skills, but with literacy being aimed at only in the standard language (Monoliterate Binlingualism), (iii) whether aural-oral fluency and literacy are to be developed in the Creole for certain types of subject-matter and in the standard language for certain other types of subject-matter (Partial Bilingualism), and (iv) whether all skills are to be developed in both Creole and standard in all domains (Full Bilingualism). There are two other alternatives that are also possible in Creole situations; these are:
>
> 3(v) whether the Creole is to be ignored completely, as has traditionally been the case in many parts of the world, and education to be attempted solely in the standard language, and (vi) whether education is to be attempted in the Creole language solely, even if at the primary level only.

Which of these alternatives a Creole-speaking community will choose will be determined by the ways in which attitudes and motivations have been influenced by the background of factors such as have been outlined in the previous sections of the paper. It has been shown, however, in Craig 1977 for example, that no matter how communities make their choices, certain generalizations seem applicable to all the Creole language situations. These generalizations are as follows: (a) in all situations, even where the professed educational policy is monolingualism in the standard language, there will be varying degrees of oral usage of Creole by indigenous children and teachers in schools; (b) there will be literacy in Creole at the primary level only in cases where there is a clear educational policy of full or partial bilingualism and such cases are rare, and (c) there will be an attempt at oral fluency and literacy in the more-extensively-acceptable standard language, at least an upper primary level, in most cases.

What seems most significant in the generalizations is the fact of the pervasiveness and persistence of oral fluency in Creole on the one hand, and an equally pervasive and persistent striving after literacy in the standard language on the other. The implication of this is that, so far as language teaching is concerned, the most common problem in all Creole situations is that of teaching a standard language (other than the Creole itself, if it has achieved such status) to Creole speakers.

The problem differs according to the two types of Creole situation discussed in Section One. If the Creole bears no significant lexical and grammatical relationship to the Standard language, then the problem of teaching the Standard is essentially that of teaching a foreign language and, as Stewart 1962 pointed out, the attitudes of the community towards Creole in such situations are generally more favourable than they would otherwise be. In such situations therefore, school programmes tend to be more realistic and more rationally designed to achieve results in terms of conferring proficiency in the standard; this happens because the child tends to be fully recognized as a foreign learner of the standard and therefore needing to be schooled within the context of one of the first four alternatives, which are clear bilingual alternatives, outlined in illustration (2) above. In this situation, the problems to be faced do not derive from the factors discussed in the sections preceding this, but are more socio-economic having to do with the underdevelopment of Creole-language communities and the poor provision of basic communal necessities, including education.

If, however, the Creole situation is of the other type, where there is significant lexical or grammatical relationship between the Creole and the Standard, then the educational problem tends to assume different proportions. The status of the child as a foreign learner of the Standard language is not likely to be clearly recognized, even though the linguistic differences between Creole and Standard will be obvious, but the traditional attitude of regarding Creole as a debased form of the Standard is likely to hinder the design and implementation of adequate educational policies; in a majority of actual cases what happens is that alternative five (see 3v., above), viz. to ignore the Creole completely in education, tends to be accepted.

However, in the latter type of situation, even if the obvious differences between the Creole and the Standard language suggest a foreign-language approach to the teaching of the standard, and therefore a bilingual type of educational programme generally, there are still likely to be special problems of the kind discussed in Craig 1976.

Firstly, apart from the attitudinal problem already referred to in respect of the relationship between the Creole and the Standard, there will tend to be a problem of low motivation in Creole-speaking children attempting to learn the standard. Part of this problem will derive from the child's perception of a relationship between the Creole language and the one the child is supposed to be learning in school; this perception has been shown (Craig 1976) to create in the child the illusion that the Standard language is already known, and the result is that child fails to obtain the equivalent of the satisfaction and learning reinforcement of the foreign learner who knows that something new has been learned and is available for use.

Another part of the motivational problem has to do with the fact that, although the age of social awareness referred to in Labov 1964 probably occurs earlier for some Creole-speaking children, judging from the early development of code-switching (Craig 1976), Creole-speaking children in the type of situation under discussion, like most non-standard speaking children attempting to learn a standard, fail to see the relevance of the Standard language to them, and fail to find any compelling reason for formally learning it. A similar phenomenon has been reported in relation to non-standard-speaking children learning English in the USA (e.g. Kochman 1969).

Still another part of the motivational problem, however, has to do with learners, in the type of situation being considered, not merely failing to see the relevance of learning the Standard language, but actually having a negative attitude to the Standard language itself, regarding it as the language of an oppressive elite, for example, or (among boys) regarding it as a language for 'sissies'. Phenomena of the latter kind have been referred to in Craig 1976 and it is clear that similar attitudes sometimes inhere in advocates of improved status for Creoles in places like Haiti, Jamaica and New Guinea.

Secondly there are problems that are largely methodological and that derive from the fact that speakers of a Creole which bears a significant lexical or grammatical relationship to the Standard are in the position of attempting to learn neither a native language nor a foreign language, but something half-way between the two when they approach the Standard. This factor has important implications for teaching methodology, and these implications have been discussed elsewhere (Craig 1976, 1977, 1978a). One particular aspect of these implications, however, is relevant here, and this is the sociological one that learners of the Standard, in the type of situation being discussed, need more than other learners to be put through processes that would sensitize them to the Standard-language requirements of different social-class roles, and condition them to Standard forms of communication when they are performing those roles. Teaching methods based on role-playing, with all their sociological and psychological implications, therefore assume particular importance in this type of situation.

Finally, in this type of situation, there are language-learning and teaching problems which have to do with the fact that the relevant learners, like some other types of non-standard speakers, are accustomed to a different format of communication from the one that is dominant in standard language. In the early work of Bernstein (e.g. 1961a, 1961b, 1961c), the kind of communication format that has since been referred to as characteristic of Creole speakers was regarded as being characteristically low-social-class and termed a restricted code, to indicate its assumed limitations as a mode of communication.

Since then in Labov 1969, Craig 1971 and elsewhere, the latter position has been disputed and even the more recent work of Bernstein (e.g. 1972) seems to take a different stand from that originally taken. What now seems apparent is that the communication format of the lower social class, including Creole speakers employs strategies that are different from the preferred ones in standard languages which have been influenced by a long tradition of written style; but the strategies of the lower-social communication format can achieve the same cognitive results as the strategies that are characteristic of standard language (Craig, in press).

The differences in communication formats that have been referred to seem to achieve added importance in the more advanced stages of language learning and language use when they can constitute significant barriers to the efficient reception and processing of information. However, they also seem to be related to wider issues that have to do with the universal conceptual structures that underlie Creole and probably all languages recently discussed in work such as Kay and Sankoff 1974; Bickerton 1977; Craig 1975, 178b. The significance of these wider issues for the sociology of language learning and teaching is that they suggest on the one hand the universal commonalities underlying the structure and the functioning of the human being, but suggest at the same time the selective procedures that are put into effect by social groupings even in relation to factors as subtle, intangible and little understood as linguistic structure.

Note

State-of-the-art paper presented in the session "The Sociology of Language Learning and Teaching" of the Ninth World Congress of Sociology, Uppsala Sweden, 14–19 August 1978. First published in *Caribbean Journal of Education*, vol. 5, no. 3.

References

Aaron, B. and Stewart, W.A. (eds.), 1969. "Linguistic-cultural differences and American education". *The Florida FL Reporter*, Anthology issue.

Adekunle, M.A. 1972. "Sociolinguistic problems in English language instruction in Nigeria". In Smith and Shuy (eds.).

Ansre, G. 1978. "Campus pidginization and accommodation in Ghana". Paper presented at the conference on *English in Non-native Contexts*, LSA Linguistic Institute, University of Illinois, July 1978.

Bailey, B.L. 1964. "Social problems in the language teaching situation in Jamaica". In *Social Dialects and Language Learning*, ed. Roger W. Shuy, Champaign, Illinois, National Council of Teachers of English.

———. 1966. *Jamaica Creole Syntax: A Transformational Approach*. Cambridge: Cambridge University Press.

Bernstein, B. 1961a. "Social structure, language and learning". *Educational Research*. 3.

———. 1961 b. "Social class and linguistic development: A theory of social learning". In *Economy, Education and Society*, ed. A.H. Halsley, J. Floud, and A. Anderson, New York: Free Press.

———. 1961c. "Aspects of language and learning in the genesis of the social process". *Journal of Child Psychology and Psychiatry* 1, 313. Reprinted pp. 251–63 in *Language, in Culture and Society*, ed. D. Hymes, New York: Harper and Row 1964.

———. 1972. "A critique of the concept of compensatory education". In Cazden, John and Hymes (eds.).

Bickerton, D. 1971. "Guyanese speech". Manuscript, University of Guyana.

———. 1973. "On the nature of a Creole continuum". *Language* 49 (3).

———. 1977. "Pidginization and creolization: Language acquisition and language universals". In Valdman (ed.).

Cassidy, F. 1961. *Jamaica Talk: 300 Years of English Language in Jamaica*. London: Macmillan.

Cazden, C.B., John, V.P. and Hymes, D. (eds.). 1972. *Functions of Language in the Classroom*. New York: Columbia University, Teachers College Press.

Craig, D. 1966. "Teaching English to Jamaican Creole speakers: A model of multi-dialect situation". *Language Learning*, 16 (1–2).

———. 1971. "Education and Creole English in the West Indies: some sociolinguistic factors". In Hymes (ed.).

———. 1974. "Developmental and social class differences in language". *Caribbean Journal of Education* 1 (2), University of the West Indies, Jamaica.

———. 1975. "A Creole English continuum and the theory of grammar". Paper presented at the International Conference on Pidgins and Creoles, University of Hawaii. To appear, Hawaii University Press.

———. 1976. "Bidialectal education: Creole and standard in the West Indies". *International Journal of the Sociology of Language*, 8, The Hague: Mouton.

———. 1977. "Creole languages and primary education". In Valdman, (ed.).

———. 1978a. "Creole and standard: partial learning, base grammar, and the mesolect". Paper presented at the Annual Roundtable Meeting, Georgetown University, Georgetown University Press.

———. 1978b. "Language education in a post-Creole society". In Spolsky and Cooper (eds.).

———. In press. *The Language Jamaican Children Speak: A Study in Social Class Distinctions*. Rowley, Massachusetts: Newbury House.

DeCamp, D. 1971. "Towards a generative analysis of a post-Creole speech continuum". In Hymes (ed.).

DeCamp, D., and Hancock, I. (eds.). 1974 *Pidgins and Creoles: Current Trends and Prospects*. Washington, DC: Georgetown University Press.

Ferguson, C. 1959. "Diglossia". *Word*, 15: 2, 325–40.

Fishman, J.A. and Lovas, J. 1970. "Bilingual education in sociolinguistic perspective". *TESOL Quarterly*, 4, 215–22.

Hancock, I.F. 1971. "A survey of the pidgins and Creoles of the world". In Hymes (ed.).

Hymes, D., (ed.). 1971. *Pidginization and Creolization of Languages*. London: Cambridge University Press.

Kay, P. and Sankoff, G. 1974. "A language-universals approach to pidgins and Creoles". In DeCamp and Hancock (eds.).

Kochman, T. 1969. "Social factors in the consideration of teaching Standard English". In Aarons and Stewart (eds.).

Labov, W. 1964. "Stages in the acquisition of Standard English". In Shuy (ed.).

———. 1969. "The logic of Non-Standard English". Twentieth Annual Roundtable Meeting. No. 22, ed. J.E. Alatis, Georgetown University, School of Languages and Linguistics.

Le Page, R., and DeCamp, D. 1960. *Jamaican Creole: An Historical Introduction*. London: Macmillan.

Pompilus, P. 1973. "Contribution á l'étude comparée du créole et du français á partir du créole haitien". *Editions Caraïbes*, Port-au-Prince, Haiti.

Rice, F.A. (ed.). 1962. *Study of the Role of Second Languages in Asia, Africa and Latin America*. Washington, DC: Center for Applied Linguistics.

Richards, J.C. 1972. "Social factors, interlanguage and language learning". *Language Learning*, 22: 2.

Rickford, J. 1974. "The insights of the mesolect". In DeCamp and Hancock (eds.).

Selinker, L. 1972. "Interlanguage." *IRAL*, 10: 3.

Sankoff, G., and Laberge, S. 1974. "On the acquisition of native speakers by a language". In DeCamp and Hancock (eds.).

Schaedel, R. (ed.) 1969. *Research and Resources of Haiti*. New York: Research Institute for the Study of Man.

Schumann, J.H. 1974. "The implications of inter-language, pidginization and creolization for the study of adult second language acquisition". *TESOL Quarterly*, 8: 2.

Smith, D.M. and Shuy, R.W. 1972. *Sociolinguistics in Cross-cultural Analysis*. Washington DC: Georgetown University Press.

Spolsky, B. and Cooper, R.L. 1978. *Case Studies in Bilingual Education*. Rowley, Massachusetts: Newbury House.

Stewart, W.A. 1962. "Creole languages in the Caribbean". In Rice (ed.).

Valdman, A. 1969. "The language situation in Haiti". In Schaedel (ed.).

———. (ed.). 1977. *Pidgin and Creole Linguistics*. Bloomington and London: Indiana University Press.

Vincent, T. 1972. "Pidgin in Nigerian literature". Paper presented at the Conference on Creole Languages and Educational Development, University of the West Indies. ALSED Programme of UNESCO, Paris.

Wurm, S.A. 1977. "Pidgins, Creoles, Lingue Frenche, and national development". In Valdman (ed.).

5 | Creole and Standard
Partial Learning, Base Grammar and the Mesolect

The principles of equality and self-determination that provide the rationale for the development of new nations and communities in contemporary times have led to the recognition that situations where Creole and standard languages coexist have to be regarded as situations requiring bilingual approaches to education. Among such situations, those where the standard language is also one of the base languages of the Creole and where a continuum of language variation between Creole and Standard has developed constitute a special subtype. The clearest examples of the latter are perhaps the officially English-speaking Caribbean and Hawaii. The sociolinguistic factors relevant to this subtype of bilingual educational situation, with particular reference to the English-official Caribbean where the presence of a language continuum makes the educational situation in the that region virtually a bidialectal one, and that, relevant to educational problems, it bears some resemblance to the social dialect situations that are the objects of concern in, for example, Stewart (1964), Shuy (1964), Baratz and Shuy (1969), Labov (1969), Wolfram (1970), and Fasold and Shuy (1970), although social conditions are different from those in North America, especially in territories where there are strong survivals of basilect Creoles.

In the English-official territories referred to, there is a growing recognition that the requirements of a quasi bidialectal education include more than merely teaching the standard dialect without inhibiting the child's home language. To be taken into consideration, for example, are the educational implications of the relationship between language and the subcultural identifications that go along with social stratification; and there are also the psycholinguistic questions that arise in relation to differences in the communicative and cognitive strategies of differently acculturated speakers in this particular societal context (Craig 1974).

An intractable problem of standard-language teaching in the English-official Caribbean situations referred to is the persistence of the interlanguage between Creole and standard that is now generally known as mesolect (Bickerton 1973; Rickford 1974). The Creole-speaking learner of the standard tends to achieve a competence in the mesolect and then seems to find an increased difficulty in moving from that point in the continuum to an achievement of competence in the standard. A partial explanation of this observation might be sought in factors that have to do with motivation and the linguistic perceptions of learners: mesolectal speakers probably find it more difficult to perceive differences between their speech and Standard English; consequently they possess a weak motivation to change their speech, and this could result in the arrest of learning; Creole speakers, on the other hand, might find it easier to perceive differences between their speech and Standard English and this might, under appropriate conditions, strengthen a motivation to change and facilitate learning up to a mesolectal level.

But the latter explanation fails to account for the fact that, in common experience all over the English-official Caribbean, it is mesolectal speakers who are most active in seeking upward social mobility through education, who seem to be most strongly motivated to achieve competence in Standard English, and who display the most frustration in the context of high failure rates in English language examinations at all levels of the school system. Clearly, the learning problems of the mesolectal speaker in progressing toward Standard English are not the result of limited interlanguage ability or motivation to learn.

Support for the latter conclusion comes from similar observations relevant to standard-language education in nonstandard speech areas in the United States. Kochman (1969), for example, points out that the 'efficiency quotient' (input vs. output) of programmes designed to teach standard dialect to non-standard speakers is extremely low. The programmes referred to tend to achieve very little in two respects; firstly, only a disappointingly small proportion of learners acquire the socially preferred forms that should (within the aims of the programmes) replace nonstandard forms; and secondly, vis-à-vis language performance, the programmes do not develop the ability to use language in the second dialect beyond what the child is already capable of doing in his native dialect.

The nonstandard dialects here referred to are similar to Caribbean English mesolectal speech in respect of their structural relationship to English; indeed, they appear to have originated in the same way as the mesolect through a process of decreolization, as suggested, for example, in Stewart (1962, 1967, 1968). It is here proposed that a common difficulty in moving from mesolect to standard is being experienced in both types of language community.

In Craig (1976), while accepting that factors relating to motivation and to interlingual perceptions – first discussed in Craig (1971) – do seem to be partly responsible for the language-learning problem just outlined, I pointed out: 'The question . . . needs to be studied whether the very nature of bidialectal situations does not produce strictly linguistic and non-attitudinal factors that have some additional bearing on the poor results of language teaching'. In the present paper, I come to the point of considering what these strictly linguistic factors might be like.

A possible explanation of the language-learning problem referred to seems to lie in the nature of the structural relationship between mesolect and Creole, on the one hand, and between mesolect and standard, on the other.

This two-way relationship with the mesolect as the centre is generally obscured, and has not so far received any attention because utterances that qualify to be regarded as mesolectal do so in two ways. First, they may qualify by containing a mixture of Creole and standard features that would not occur simultaneously in either Creole or standard.

For example, the sentences in (1) (Rickford 1974: 94), taken in each case as a whole, are mesolectal although, with the exception of e, all the features underlined in them are basilectal Creole features.

(1) She must be <u>da</u> hunt husband.
            a
    'She must be hunting for a husband.'

I <u>done</u> <u>de</u> <u>de</u>
   b   c d
'I am already there.'

I <u>ain't</u> know <u>se</u> y'all <u>bin</u> gone
  e   f   g
'I didn't know that you all had gone.'

However, sentences may qualify to be regarded as mesolectal, second, by virtue of their containing features that are absent from both basilect Creole and the standard language as in (2) (Rickford 1974: 100), where the underlined features, except probably <u>b</u>, are peculiar to the mesolect.

(2)   But I <u>doz</u> go to see people when <u>they sick.</u>
         a   b
       'But I usually go to see people when they're sick.'

       He <u>doz be</u> up and cut wood sometimes . . .
            c

       'He generally gets up and cuts wood sometimes . . .'

Rickford (ibid.) demonstrates the necessity for the latter type of feature to be studied in its own right, and he goes further to conclude that that particular mesolectal item in the last mentioned examples: <u>doz</u>

> . . . whether borrowed from Irish English, or early Modern English, clearly represents a form of calquing on a grammatical semantic category that existed previously. It adds to a growing store of knowledge that calquing – both lexical and grammatical – plays an important role in all the major transition periods of a Creole's life history . . .

It would seem that the preceding conclusion relative to <u>doz</u> is correct not only for that item, but that it can be generalized to provide a surprisingly obvious explanation, as will be shown subsequently, for such mesolectal features as are peculiar to the mesolect. If this is the case, then on the way towards seeking a complete explanation of the language-learning problem earlier referred to, one should seek to account for the following:

(3a)   The early replacement of some basilectal Creole features by standard-language ones.

(3b)   The persistence of peculiarly mesolectal features that tend to fossilize in nonstandard speakers.

(3c)   The persistence of some basilectal Creole features in the mesolect.

The rest of this paper first examines the suggestion relative to mesolectal calquing and the issues stated in (3), and then considers some implications for standard-language learning and teaching in relevant situations.

The most conclusive evidence that is possible concerning the nature of peculiarly mesolectal utterances or relevant portions of such utterances compare in semantactic structure (SS) with the corresponding structure of the Creole and standard-language equivalents. Such an analysis of a representative set of items is shown in (4).

It has been remarked before this – as, for example, in Bickerton (1971) – that the English-language 'mistakes' of Creole-influenced speakers of English, even when they are not exactly Creole in morphology, can be shown to be derived directly from the structure of Creole; but reasons for the phenomena stated in (3) and the related suggestions relative to mesolectal calquing are yet to be looked at systematically. First of all, using the examples in (4) to begin with, we may look at the mesolectal utterances for complete standard-language replacements of Creole items. Wherever replacements occur, it may be noted that they are of the kinds shown in (4).

(4)		Creole	Mesolect	Standard
i.	Item	/ . . . fi–mi buk / (JC)	/ . . . mi buk / No particle.	' . . . my book'
	SS	Particle to indicate possession.	Word order only.	Inflection of first NP.
ii.	Item	/a (fi–mi buk)/ (JC)	/iz (mi buk) /	'It's (my book)'
	SS	Front-shifting of verb-particle to achieve focus on an NP.	Same as Creole with relexification of verb particle.	Impersonal pronoun 'it' + copula.
iii.	Item	/a kot yu kot i/	/iz kot yu kot it/	'What you have done is cut it.'
	SS	Same as (ii) with verb front shifted and reduplicated as well so as to achieve focus on verb.	Same as Creole.	Split sentence construction.
iv.	Item	/mi bin . . ./ (GC)	(a) /a(i) biin. . ./ (b) /a(i) did go . . ./	'I went . . . ,
	SS	Invariant pronoun + substantive-verb – /bin/	(a) Same as creole except for subject form of pronoun and anglicized phonology of /bin/. (b) Relexification of /bin / by English 'go' but with introduction of the creole particle for PAST.	First person, nominative case of pronoun with verb inflected to show PAST.
v.	Item	'we bin duh nyam . . .' (Stewart 1968; Rickford 1974) Pronoun + PAST + CONTINUATIVE + Verbs.	'we was eatin . . .'	'we were eating'
	SS		Pronoun + PAST + Relexified verb + CONTINUATIVE 'ing'.	Pronoun + PAST + Verbal-plural + Verb + CONTINUATIVE 'ing.'
vi.	Item	'I stay eat' (Tzuzaki 1971) Pronoun + CONTINUATIVE + Substantive verb.	(a) 'I stay eating' (b) 'I eating'	'I am eating'
	SS		(a) Pronoun + Creole-CONTINUATIVE + Verb-with-continuative-inflection. (b) Pronoun + Verb-with continuative-inflection.	Pronoun + TENSE – present + Verb-with-continuative inflection.
vii.	Item	/mi na (en) gat non/ (JC) (bin) (GC)	got /a neva get non/ duon in	'I haven't got any' 'I didn't get any'
	SS	Pronoun + NEG (+PAST) + Substantive–verb + Indefinite–negative– pronoun.	Pronoun + NEG + Substantive-verb + Indefinite-negative-pronoun.	Pronoun + TENSE – past + NEG +Substantive – Verb + Indefinite-indeterminate– pronoun.
viii.	Item	/(a) we i de?/ im	/wier i iz?/ weer	'Where is he?'
	SS	Question indicated by intonation.	Same as creole.	Question indicated by intonation as well as reversal of S–V order.

(5a) Phonological change in the direction of Standard English, e.g.

gat –>	got/get	(4vii)
we –>	wier/weer	(4viii)
bin –>	biin*	(4iii)
i –>	it	(4iv)

*(Through the influence of written English, though semantically this is still not standard)

(5b) Relexification that does not involve syntactic change, e.g.

nyam –> 'eat'		(4v)

(5c) Some differentiation in pronominal morphology with the exclusion of the possessive, e.g.

mi –>	'I/me'	(4iv)
		(4vii)

But note also:

mi = 'my'		(4i)

Further examples, apart from these, of such early replacement of Creole features by completely standard ones are, of course, numerous within the language community: replacement of Creole low, back /a/ by some higher vowel in items such as /gaan/ 'gone', /mada/ 'mother', and so on; reflexifications such as /juk/ 'stick' (verb), /lik/ 'hit'. And so on; and pronominal differentiation such as he/ she, him/her, they/them, where there was no differentiation such as he/she, him/her, they/them, where there was no differentiation before. It is to be noted, however, and it will be referred to subsequently, that these types of early, mesolectal changes in the direction of Standard English are of little transformational depth. The most considerable change in terms of such depth is in pronouns, but it is very significant that is it the possessive form (in pronouns as well as in nouns) which, in theory, is more complex than the others, which tends to remain invariant as in Creole.

Next, we may examine in (4) those features that appear to be peculiarly mesolectal and that do not belong to either basilect Creole or standard language. Included in this set are features that involve the transference of a Creole semantactic strategy to utterances that would otherwise be Standard English. The features in the whole set are of the following types.

(6a) Zero replacement of a creole item, e.g.

fi –>	Ø	(4i)
stay–>	Ø	(4vi)

(6b) Calquing of a creole item by an item used differently in Standard
English, e.g.

a	->	iz	(4ii; 4iii)
de	->	iz	(4viii)
ma	->	neva	
		duon	
		in	(4vii)
Ø-PAST	->	di (d)	(4iv)
bin duh	->	invariant	(4v)
		'was'	

(6c) Persistence of a creole semantactic strategy with Standard-English
lexis, e.g.

Fronting of verb-particle to show focus on a following NP	(4ii)
Fronting of verb-particle + substantive-verb and reduplication of the verb to show focus on a VP	(4iii)
Double negation	(4vii)
Invariant word order for statement and question	(4viii)

Again, it is understood that further examples of the same types will not be difficult to find within the language community. What is significant about these
types of item is that, in nature, they derive from virtually the same process as
that noted at (5b): relexification without syntactic change.

It seems clear, then, that changes in the direction of Standard English that
appear in the mesolect are predominately either phonological or, like Rickford's
doz, are direct lexifications of grammatical semantic elements that are explicit
in Creole. This explains the phenomena referred to in (3a) and (3b). By implication, this explains (3c) as well, since it can be expected that Creole items within
the competence of any speaker that cannot be phonologically modified or cannot be relexified will persist as Creole. The nature of such items will be more
fully discussed subsequently.

It is now possible to see, therefore, why Creole-speaking learners of Standard
English find it relatively easy to move to a mesolectal level, but thereafter find it
increasingly difficult to move beyond that; and why nonstandard speakers who
are already at the equivalent of a mesolectal level tend to remain there without
significant change. The reasons are as follows. Up to the mesolectal level, the
semantactic processes and strategies being performed by the learner are exactly
the same as or closely like those that are habitual in Creole, so difficulties of
Creole-speaking learners of the standard, like those of the nonstandard speakers

generally, are minimal. After this stage, however, a new order of difficulty begins to be experienced; and it is the nature of this order of difficulty that now merits discussion.

If we accept that concepts are events which, somehow or other, occur in the human mind, and that language is a means of labelling concepts (see, for example, Chafe 1970: 17), then the question at issue is: how do the labelling processes of Creole or mesolect differ from those of standard language, as we must assume they do in view of the learning difficulty just discussed?

This question and the assumptions relevant to it assume in turn that there are 'universals of cognitive structure and process that underlie all human language ability and language use' (Kay and Sankoff 1974: 62). But such universals, precisely because they concern conceptual structure or conceptual knowledge itself, and not just how the elements within that structure or knowledge are labelled in language, cannot be sought as universals of language in the way Kay and Sankoff (ibid.) suggested. Bickerton's (1977) criticism of the latter, therefore, seems correct in this respect although, by subsequently suggesting that 'the human faculté de langage . . . must . . . contain some kind of analog for the instructions "if your input language has no nonpunctual aspect marker, employ a locative expression preverbally . . ."', and so on, Bickerton (1977: 64) is, in fact, committing the same error he criticized, of assuming the universals of underlying structure to be far less abstract than they can possibly be.

The nature of underlying conceptual or cognitive structure or of conceptual knowledge, however, is, to begin with, an epistemological question; how elements within such structure or knowledge are labelled is, on the other, a linguistic question; and an investigation of one type of question entails an investigation of the other. Some discussion that relates such enquiry to the description of the competence of speakers in a Creole-language continuum is to be found in Craig (1975), and the kind of grammar that such an enquiry justifies is outlined in Craig (1978).

What is important for the present is to consider how the two main assumptions accepted in the first two paragraphs of this section of the paper might elucidate the question posed in the first paragraph. The two assumptions may be restated as follows:

(7a) The structure of conceptual knowledge is the same for all human beings.

(7b) Language is a means of labelling concepts.

If these two assumptions are correct, then the conceptual and linguistic knowledge of speakers in relation to any meaningful segment of any language are related and have a general structure as diagrammed in (8).

What is suggested in (8) is that, when concepts occur in the mind, they may possibly be given direct one-to-one labels in terms of lexis and syntax simultaneously. This would then be the first level of language, and it is theorized that if an output of sentences is made at this level, that output would have the simplest possible syntactic structure and lexis. After Level-1, transformational processes involving the movement, deletion, and grouping of already theoretically existing labels and the relabelling (lexicalization) of the grouped meanings may be successively applied on the linguistic string, and this produces increasingly more complex levels of lexis and syntax from Level-2 to a possible Level-n. An actual linguistic output could be made by a speaker at any level, depending on the conventions of his particular language and his individual conditioning in terms of the use of that language, but at each succeeding level the meanings expressed would be identical with those originally existing at Level-1.

The preceding notion of the grammatical results of the relationship between conceptual knowledge and language ought, logically to have been the central theme of the type of enquiry termed 'generative semantics', following as it did on the pioneering work of Chomsky (1957, 1965). However, that type of enquiry, despite its many insights as exemplified in Lakoff (1971), McCawley (1968), Bach (1968), and Postal (1970) has failed to provide an explanation of language, precisely because it has ignored the link between epistemology and linguistic theory and concentrated instead on a theorized link with logic. These issues are further treated in Craig (1978).

If the preceding theoretical orientation is correct, even without its further elaboration at this time, we are in a position to understand the nature of the difference between Creole or mesolectal language and standard language. All investigators agree on the lexical and syntactic simplicity of the former as compared with the latter. In the light of the theory just proposed, this simplicity stems from the fact that Creole is a linguistic output made at an earlier level (i.e. in terms of the hypotheses in (8)) than standard language characteristically is. Conceptually or cognitively and semantically, however, the two types of language have the same base preceding as at Level-1.

We may note at this point that the first unclarity about simplification in language has to do with theories of linguistic and cognitive deficit in speakers of nonstandard languages, pidgins and Creoles, or lower social class speakers generally. Labov (1969) has settled the question in one way, but within the notions here proposed it is clear that the cognitive-conceptual base of the mentioned types of speakers has to be regarded as the same as that of any types of speakers; suggestions such as those in the early work of Bernstein (e.g. 1961a, 1961b, 1961c) are therefore seen to have no foundation in theory, even without empirical contradictions such as those indicated in Craig (1974).

(8)   Potential linguistic structure of any meaningful segment of any language.

Conceptual events in the mind:

Level-1 Language: Possible labels (lexical and syntactic) that represent the immediate conceptual knowledge of speakers.

Level-2 Language: Possible derived labels expressing the same meaning as in Level 1.

Level-3 Language: Possible further derived labels expressing the same meanings as in Levels 1 and 2.

Level-n Language: Possible n-times derived labels expressing the same meanings as in Levels 1–n-1.

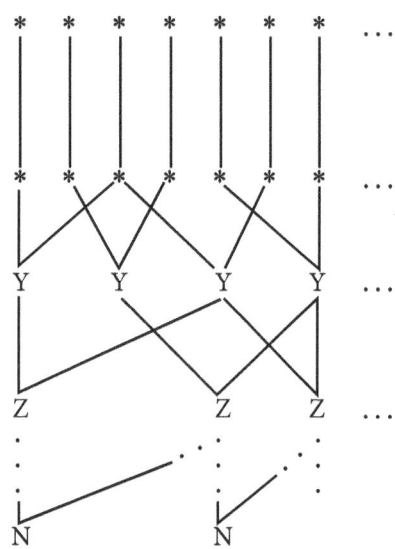

The second unclarity that can be dispelled at this point has to do with the vague suggestions often made in recent times about a human language facility, a universal base language, and so on, as if these things exist independently of any specific language. What the notions in this paper unequivocally propose is that there is a base grammar of every language, and that base grammar is the same for all languages.

After Level-1 (as in 8, once again), not only would all languages successively increase in grammatical and lexical complexity, but each language could possibly adopt sets of intermediate-level grammatical alternatives, with resulting surface consequences that could be peculiar to itself; this would account for grammatical diversity as well as similarity between languages.

In these terms, the nature of the differences between Creole or mesolect and standard language, and consequently, the learner of the standard, may be summarized as follows

(9)   i. Choice of different grammatical alternatives in the two language systems after Level-1.
     ii. Choice of an earlier level (whichever this might be) for a linguistic output in Creole or mesolect than for one in standard language.
    iii. Consequent upon (ii), continuation of the following procedures after the output level of Creole or mesolect has been reached:
        (a) Making of new segmentations in any given string of meanings, if higher-level labels for those segmentations exist in the lexicon.
        (b) In effecting (a), conservation of existing syntactic relationships and of the speaker's intentions of focusing on specific meanings in the existing string of meanings.
        (c) Relabelling with new lexis (lexicalization) of the segmentations identified at (a).
        (d) Simultaneously with (c), insertion of syntactic markers and focusing conventions consistent with (b).

It might be noted, in passing, although the argument cannot be developed here, that if Creole or mesolect as well as standard language could have been conceived of as characteristically achieving a linguistic output at the same level in terms of (8), then a different analysis would be necessary in (9) after (9i); the situation then would be the same as would have to be assumed for two standard or long evolved languages with outputs at the same levels of labelling.

Some empirical characteristics of Creole and standard that support the analysis in (9) and the conclusions that precede it can easily be perceived; and these characteristics are the source of the standard- language-learning difficulty of Creole or mesolectal speakers. The categorization of these characteristics in terms of the analysis at (9) has the advantage of indicating the relationship between their grammatical status and the underlying cognitive structure of language. Discussion of the characteristics thus categorized follows.

The difference in choices referred to in (9i) as following after Level-1 can be seen in the grammatical alternatives shown in (10). This list consists of all the categories of items which Bickerton (1974) identifies as universals of early-creolized Creoles. Within the theoretical notions here advanced, the question as to whether these similarities derive from the closeness of Creoles to the universal conceptual base of language would be settled conclusively by a description of what has here been referred to as Level-1. Such a description, as pointed out already, is beyond our present purposes, but grammatical similarities between Creoles strengthen the probability that the stated theoretical notions are right. We could add to the similarities already stated some other ones such as invariant word order for statement and question and the use of particles as a labelling device where standard language tends to use inflections.

(10)

	Creole choice	Standard Choice
i. 'Generic' categorization indicated in nouns by:	Ø – article, e.g. /daag baak/	Pluralization, e.g. 'dogs bark'
ii. Tense and aspect indicated in verb by:	Preverbal invariant particles, e.g. (4v)	Inflection of the main verb and variant auxiliary verbs, e.g. (4v)
iii. Focussing of either NP or VP indicated by:	Front shifting (with VP reduplication in the case of VP focussing), e.g. (4ii) and (4iii)	Predication after impersonal 'it + be' or split-sentence construction, e.g. (4ii) and (4iii)
iv. Statement of attribute, location, existence by:	Copula differentiation, e.g. /im de outsaid/ */im a outsaid/ /im outsaid/ /im a man/ */im de man/	Use of 'be' in all cases 'he is outside' 'he is a man'
v. Negation by:	Multiple marking, e.g. (4vii)	Single marking, e.g. (4vii)

The next set of empirical characteristics that support the analysis in (9) are relevant to the notions in (9ii) and (9iii)

(11)   i. In order to realize (9iiia) and (9iiic), the production of a 'higher order' type of lexis that includes derived nominals generally, and abstract nominals and adjectives that characteristically carry a +human restriction, such as sincere/sincerity, trustworthy/trustworthiness, idlesome, careful, suspicious . . . and so on.

ii. In order to realize (9iiib) and (9iiid), relatively high usage of devices such as inflection purely to show syntactic and semantic relationships between lexical items that are already labelled as semantic entities, e.g. the inflection of a verb to show 'plural' in agreement with a plural NP, and the '-ing' suffix of a verb to show continuative, although that element is already labelled by the concatenation of 'be' and the verb.

iii. Because of (i) and also because (ii) makes it feasible, the use of longer rather than the shorter sentences with a relatively higher proportion of phrasally complex sentences.

These empirical consequences become evident in the further comparison of Creole and standard. As characteristics, they are absent from Creole, since Creole is lexicalized at a level where they are unnecessary, but they are present in standard language. Those referred to in (11ii) can clearly be seen in standard language equivalents of Creole utterances such as those given in (4). Those referred to in (11i) can be seen when it becomes obligatory in translations of Creole utterances to use standard language lexis which is nonexistent in Creole, but of which the meanings seem to be analytically represented in the Creole originals; for example:

(12) i. /iz afta da da waata staat iitin/
        'It was after that that erosion set in'
        (literally: is after that the water start eating)
        Bickerton (1973: 654) (My underlying and and comment in paranthesis)

      ii. ii. /im no miin notin im se/
          'He's not sincere'
          (literally: him not mean nothing him say)

      iii. /na len im no moni, im tel lai an im tiif/
          'Don't lend him any money, he's untrustworthy'
          (literally: . . . him tell lie and him thief (i.e.) steal))

Those characteristics referred to in (11iii) would also, again, be absent from Creole but more frequently present in standard language, and particularly standard language that has been influenced over time by the written, literate, norm. The reason why the characteristics tend to be absent from Creole is that, as implied already in both (9) and (11), the paucity of explicit labelling of purely syntactic relationships and the stringent reduction of redundancy in labelling that is characteristic of Creole (all of which is theoretically accounted for, as already explained) require that sentences be kept in relatively short strings unified by single, unexpanded noun phrases, similar verb phrases, and coordinate linking as often as necessary. Deriving from this is the typical staccato phrasing of Creole language discourse, illustrated in (13) and (14) with sentences and also what could be taken in theory as rudimentary sentences separated, for clarity, by the mark 'Λ'.

(13)   Pes pikinini Λ ia bai yu go wok long, Λ bai yu stap ia Λ na bai yu stap long banis kau Λ bilong mi Λ na bai taim mi dai Λ bai yu lukautim Λ na yu save wokim susu Λ na bai yu givim long, Λ women ia, Λ stua, Λ bai ol i baim.
'You, first son, will go and work in, you'll stay on my cattle farm and when I die you'll look after it, and you'all keep milking them and you'll send it to the store, and the people will buy it.'
(Sankoff and Laberge 1974: 80)

(14)   Im bwail di hat korsiin pan a parij, Λ an im tek out fi im Λ an gi Bra Anansi de balans. Λ Bra Anansi ties i. Λ So wen i bon Bra Anansi so, Λ Bra Anansi se: Λ Laad, Λ Bra Aligeta, Λ a disaya yu kaal hat, Λ man? Λ Mek mi put i out a son Λ an mek I likl hata. Λ Den a stor i miinwail, Λ den mek i likl hata. Λ Wen im put i out de, Λ a stor i, Λ a stor i, Λ dat taim it a kuol, Λ miinwail a kuol. Λ Den miinwail im stor, Λ wen im ties it, Λ an si se Λ i kuol, Λ im se: Λ Laad, Λ Bra Aligeta, Λ a nou I hat. Λ An im dis pik op i Λ an mek so, Λ wups. Λ dat finish nou. (from Bailey 1971: 347)
'He boiled the hot kerosene pan of porridge, and he took out his and gave Bra Anansi the balance. Bra Anansi tasted it. So when it burned Bra Nansi so, Bra Anansi said: Lord, Bra Alligator, is it this you call hot, man? Let me put it out in the sun and make it little hotter. Then (I will) stir it meanwhile, then make it a little hotter. Then (I will) stir it meanwhile, then make it a little hotter. When he put it out there, stirring it, stirring it, that time it was cooling, meanwhile cooling. Then while he was stirrin, when he tasted it and saw that it was cool, he said: Lord, Bra Alligator, it is now that it is hot. And he just picked it up, and did so, woops. That is finished now.'

The fact that the procedures referred to in (9iii) and their empirical conse-quences outlined in (11) are present in standard language, but absent in Creole has the following result: when Creole and mesolectal speakers attempt to pro-duce standard language, they tend to make a type of mistake that results from their general inability to extend and hold grammatical relationships across sen-tence boundaries. Mistakes of this type include those which Burt and Kiparsky (1974) refer to as 'global' mistakes and which are recognized as being more seri-ous barriers to communication than other types of mistakes that such speakers might make.

The global mistakes, as could be predicted from (9iii) and (11) involve S-V-O order (Creole and mesolectal speakers aiming to produce standard language often omit necessary parts of this order in longer sentences), use of standard language connectors: but, because, although, etc. (the Creole use of and with appropriate sentences often provides the normal equivalents of these to which the learners are accustomed), distinctions between coordinate and relative clause constructions, parallel structure in reduced coordinate clauses, and tense continuity across clauses.

From all of the preceding, in brief, it seems clear that the Creole or mes-olectal speaker learning a standard language faces a special difficulty. This dif-ficulty, together with Creole language universals and the relationship between Creole and standard, can be explained, to an extent not otherwise possible, by a notion of grammar which hypothesizes that all language derives from a com-mon conceptual base and then develops through progressively more complex levels of labelling. Differentiation between languages exists because alternative grammatical choices become increasingly possible across the successive levels of labelling. Creole as a language system makes a linguistic output at an earlier level of labelling than standard does. The consequence of this is that Creole or mesolectal speakers learning a standard language are required to carry out the procedures outlined at (9) to an extent which their native language system seldom, if ever, requires.

In relation to standard language teaching in Creole or mesolectal situations, the conclusions so far arrived at in this paper permit some supplementation to the factors and procedures discussed in Craig (1971, 1976). Those procedures merit some repetition to begin with.

The standard language knowledge of the Creole or mesolectal speaker, for the purpose of structuring a teaching programme, is considered as consisting of sets of structures that are common to both standard and nonstandard speech (Class A structures), sets that would be produced by the learner only in standard language prestige or stress situations (Class B structures), sets which the learner would recognize and comprehend if used by other speakers, but which the learner him/herself would be unable to produce (Class C structures), and sets that would be totally unknown to the learner (Class D structures). The teaching programme dictated by this categorization of standard language vis-à-vis the learner and by the considerations related to the categorization is structured as in the following summary from Craig (1976: 111).

1. Topics for treatment in language are selected so as to reflect the interests, maturity, and immediate cultural environment of the learners, but at the same time so as to permit adequate use of the specific linguistic structures that form the goal of teaching at the specific point in time.

2. The learners are led by the teacher to explore the topic fully in whatever language the learners possess. The teacher may either speak the vernacular, or speak some other type of language closer to the standard or speak the standard itself, so long as the learners are able to comprehend easily; and the teacher accepts whatever language the learners choose to respond in, including such new language as is infiltrating into the learners' competence. This part of the programme is completely oral and may be designated 'free talk'.

   The purpose of this part is to promote normal growth and development of the learners in whatever language medium is most natural to them.

3. The teacher uses the selected topic, or aspects of the topic, as the basis of systematic quasi-foreign language practice. Because of the high rate of recognition and comprehension in the bidialectal situation, through the learners' possession of the language strata A, B, and C, teaching procedures do not usually call for a very intensive use of imitation drills, but rather more for substitution and transformation practices, controlled dialogues and dramas, and a heavy reliance on simulated situations for forcing learners into a creative use of the specific linguistic structures that are aimed at. This part of the programme may be designated 'controlled talk' and only standard language is used.

4. For teaching in (3), linguistic structures are selected so that, relevant to the A, B, C, D classification of structures already discussed, the learners are forced to use a target structure or target structures selected from C or D (which for practical purposes may be combined into a single class),

and at the same time to use incidental structures which come fortuitously from A and B (which, again for practical purposes, may also be combined into a single class).

5. Language learners who are also learning to read use material consisting only of such linguistic structures as they have already learned at each given stage, as at (3), and that are relevant to the topics discussed at (2). Language learners who can already read may use materials that are linguistically unstructured (and the more such learners can be saturated with reading, the better). The purpose of this set of measures is to ensure that the acquisition of and interest in reading, is not hampered by standard language deficiencies, and that reading and language-learning should reinforce each other; once reading is firmly acquired, however, there is no longer any point in linking it to the formal learning of language structure.

6. For all learners, use is made in writing only of those linguistic structures that have already been learned as at (3), and in most cases the content of the writing is restricted to topics treated as at (2). By this means, writing is closely linked to proficiency in speech, and one reinforces the other.

7. The various subject areas of the total school curriculum enter into the selection of topics explained as at (1) so that aspects of these areas get reworked in controlled speech, reading, and writing in the same way as all other experiences.

The supplementation to these procedures that now seems to be indicated needs to consist of methods for habituating learners in the spontaneous and subconscious performance of the types of task suggested in (9iii) and the consequent achievement of the results specified in (11). This is not the first time that such procedures have been suggested as necessary for learners of the types being considered here; but previous suggestions have arrived at the stated conclusions from somewhat different premises that mainly have to do with observed differences between the communication styles of upper and lower social class speakers in language-continua situations. Such procedures, for example, are outlined in Craig (1972), where the difference in communication styles that seemed to justify them were for the first time linked to a theory of language similar to, though less explicitly formulated than, the one suggested here and in Craig (1978). The procedures involve getting learners to take what might otherwise be terminal standard language strings, but at the level of lexical and syntactic complexity at which Creole or mesolect would make an output, and learning to proceed through the transformations that would take these strings to a later level of output as in literate standard language. For most Creole or mesolectal learners, this type of learning is necessary for efficient production of standard language, but even if it is considered to be not crucial from the standpoint of language production, it certainly seems to have an important bearing on the reception of standard language.

> Without such learning, many originally non-standard speakers who succeed in mastering the basic morphology and syntax of the Standard operate at a relatively low receptive level, a fact which seldom becomes evidenced until such speakers begin to experience the demands of higher education. (Craig 1976: 125)

The focal point of the discussion in this paper is the interrelationship between conceptualization, language structure, and language learning, and how this interrelationship is to be represented in a unified theory. The study of standard language learning in a continuum situation involving Creole and Standard is a small opening into this vast field.

References

Bach, E. 1968. "Nouns and noun phrases". In: Bach and Harms, eds.

Bach, E., and R. Harms. 1968. *Universals in Linguistic Theory*. New York: Holt, Rinehart and Winston.

Bailey, B. 1971 . "Jamaican Creole: Can dialect boundaries de defined?" In: Hymes, ed.

Baratz, J. , and R.W. Shuy, eds. 1969. *Teaching Black Children to Read*. Washington, DC: Center for Applied Linguistics.

Bernstein, B. 1961a. "Social structure, language and learning". *Educational Research 3*.

———. 1961b. "Social class and linguistic developmental: A theory of social learning." In: *Economy, Education and Society*. Edited by A.H. Halsey, J. Floud, and A. Anderson. New York New York: The Free Press.

———. 1961c. "Aspects of language and learning in the genesis of the social process". *Journal of Child Psychology and Psychiatry* 1 (313). Reprinted in: *Language, Culture and Society*, D. Hymes. 251–63.

Bickerton, D. 1971. "Guyanese speech". Ms. University of Guyana.

———. 1973. "On the nature of a Creole continuum". *Lanugage* 49 (3).

———. 1977. "Pidginization and creolization: Language acquisition and language universals". In: Valdman, ed.

Burt, M., and C. Kiparsky. 1974. "Global and local mistakes". In: Schumann and Stenson, eds. 71–80.

Chafe, W. 1970. *Meaning and the structure of language*. Chicago and London: University of Chicago Press.

Craig, D.R. 1971. "Education and Creole English in the West Indies: Some sociolinguistic factors". In: Hymes, ed.

———. 1972. "Intralingual differences, communication and language theory". In: *Proceedings of the Conference on Creole Languages and Educational Development*. Paris: UNESCO.

———. 1974. "Developmental and social class differences in language". *Caribbean Journal of Education* 1: 5–23. University of the West Indies, Jamaica.

———. 1975. "A Creole language continuum and the theory of grammar". In: *Proceedings of the International Conference on Pidgins and Creoles*. Edited by Derek Bickerton and Richard R. Day. Honolulu: University of Hawaii Press.

———. 1976. "Bidialectal education: Creole and standard in the West indies". *International Journal of the Sociology of Language* 8: 94–134.

———. 1978. "Lexical meaning". University of the West Indies, Jamaica. Mimeo.

DeCamp, D., and I. Hancock, eds. 1974. *Pidgins and Creoles: Current trends and prospects*. Washington, DC: Georgetown University Press.

Fasold, R.R., and R.W. Shuy, eds. 1970. *Teaching Standard English in the inner city*. Arlington, VA: Center for Applied Linguistics.

Hymes, D., ed. 1971. *Pidginization and creolization of language*. Cambridge: Cambridge University Press.

Kay, P., and G. Sankoff. 1974. "A language-universals approach to pidgin and Creoles". In: DeCamp and Hancock, eds.

Kochman, T. 1969. "Social factors in the consideration of teaching Standard English". *The Florida Foreign Language Reporter, 7*.

Labov, W. 1969. "The logic of non-Standard English". In: *Georgetown University Round Table on Languages and Linguistics 1969*. Edited by James E. Alatis. Washington, DC: Georgetown University Press. 1–43.

Lakoff, G. 1971. *Syntactic irregularity*. New York: Holt, Rinehart and Winston.

McCawley, J. 1968. "Lexical insertion in a transformational grammar without deep structure". *Papers from the Fourth Regional Meeting*, Chicago Linguistics Society. 71–80.

Postal, P. 1970. "On the surface verb 'Remind'". *Linguistic Enquiry* 1 (1): 37–120.

Rickford, J. 1974. "The insights of the mesolect". In: DeCamp and Hancock, eds.

Sankoff, G., and S. Laberge. 1974. "On the acquisition of native speakers by a language". In: DeCamp Hancock, eds.

Schumann, J., and N. Stenson, eds. 1974. *New frontiers in second language learning*. Rowley, MA: Newbury House.

Shuy, R.W., ed. 1964. "Social dialects and language in the Caribbean". In: Rice, ed.

Stewart, W.A. 1962. "Creole languages in the Caribbean". In: Rice, ed.

———, ed. 1964. "Non-standard speech and the teaching of English". Washington, DC: Center for Applied Linguistics.

———. 1967. "Sociolinguistic factors in the history of American Negro dialects". *The Florida Foreign Language Reporter* 5 (2).

———. 1968. "Continuity and change in American Negro dialects". *Foreign Language Reporter* 6 (1).

Tsuzaki, S. 1971. "Coexistent systems in language variation: The case of Hawaiian English". In: Hymes, ed.

Valdman, A., ed. 1977. *Pidgin and Creole linguistics*. Bloomington and London: Indiana University Press.

Wolfram, W. 1970. "Sociolinguistic alternatives in teaching reading to non-standard speakers". *Research Quarterly* 6 (1).

6

English Language Teaching

Problems and Prospects in the West Indies

Over thirty years ago, in the first formal study of reading achievement in the English-official Caribbean, Walters (1957) had this to say about language in Jamaican schools:

> Although the children were using chiefly English words, the structure of their sentences and the idiom used was by no means English. In short, English words are used in an order and combination which produces what we have called 'Jamaican Creole'. . . The implications of this for the teaching of reading and of written and spoken English, is that children have to learn, not new words, but a new way of arranging them. The general attitude to this problem has been that Jamaican Creole structure is wrong and must be corrected . . . A gradual change of attitude is being noted, however, when teachers are warned not to begin corrections too early and so stifle spontaneity. A further step takes us away from the concept of "correcting wrong speech", towards learning a new way of saying things. (Walters, 1957: 39–40)

Walters was merely reflecting educated opinion at that time, informed by description of Jamaican Creole speech such as can be seen in Le Page (1957–58), Le Page and DeCamp (1960), Bailey (1966) and Cassidy (1961). However, what was then being said about Jamaican speech could also have been said without much modification about language in most parts of the so-called

English-speaking Caribbean including parts such as Saint Lucia and Dominica where French Creole is additionally spoken.[1]

Whatever we might think today about the earlier speech descriptions, idealistic and failing to reflect the wide range of language variation that can be found in the community, as they are now held to be, they stimulated in educational circles a certain awareness. This awareness is perhaps most significantly noticeable in the curriculum guides that have been coming out of the ministries of education since Walters, where teachers were urged to allow children to retain their Creole speech (contrary to the policy of repression, even if they veiled sometimes, that prevailed previous to this), and to teach them English by showing that there was 'a new way of saying things.'

This recognition of English as 'a new way' and not the only way of saying things represented an improvement on previous practice. It did not succeed, however, as it ought to have done, in forcing a majority of teacher supervisors, trainers and classroom teachers of the Language Arts and English to take seriously the advances that have occurred in the world at large in the teaching of second languages and second dialects, and to use these advances in the teaching of English.

What it did lead to, or in some cases merely perpetuated, was a method (if it can be called a method) of teaching English by *correction.*

The teachers waited until the children produced the Creole forms (otherwise known as 'errors' or 'mistakes') when English was required, and then took time off either immediately or subsequently to show the children 'a new way', that is to say 'an English way' of saying or writing these forms. Needless to say, this approach to the teaching of English cannot but be futile, because it is of necessity haphazard and provides no systematic reinforcement of anything that the learner is taught.

At present, three decades after Walters, many educators have not moved beyond teaching by correction in their perception of what second-language or second-dialect methods mean or could mean in the English-official Caribbean. Some reasons for, and consequences of this will be commented on below. In the meantime, it remains amazingly true to say that many educators in a position to influence the teaching of English and the Language Arts, while willing to admit that English, if not a foreign language, is certainly not the native language of the vast majority of Jamaican or other children in the English-official Caribbean, continue to champion a native-language approach to the teaching of English.

A striking example of this was provided recently. An obviously highly regarded reviewer, who nevertheless remains anonymous to this writer, in considering the English-teaching needs of that vast majority of English-based, Creole-speaking children who at age 12 fail to gain entry into high schools, expressed a preference for the immediate depth and relative sophistication of a totally native-language English-teaching approach. The reviewer had high praise for a textbook series that exemplifies such an approach, and found that an added merit of the series was that "*furthermore common Caribbean errors are used in grammar correction exercises.*" The reviewer found on the other hand that, in an alternative series with a second-dialect approach, the initial simplicity, gradual and systematic attention to the teaching of English syntax, and phased introduction of language-usage skills over the first few years was totally inadequate and unsatisfactory.

In relation to classroom procedures in English teaching in the Jamaican or English-official Caribbean context, the reviewer apparently saw no need for the further education of teachers, but claimed approvingly that "*teachers still rely substantially on traditional English texts, and the classical approach to language teaching is still very much alive. On the other hand, one notable observation is that many teachers agree that the translation of Creole sentences, dialogues and passages to English, could help in the extension of expression skills.*"

The praise of mere translation, in the absence of procedures for the systematic teaching of the language into which the translation is to take place, to say the least, betrays a lack of understanding of a how a new language is learned.

And there are other deficiencies of understanding which accompany this idea, and which have serious consequences for the practices and materials which those who supervise and lead are promoting in the schools. One of the most serious of these is the lack of understanding that there is a hierarchy of language-usage skills. A second-language or a second-dialect approach has to observe this hierarchy and be guided by it. A native-language approach, however, as in the "traditional English texts" referred to by the reviewer can ignore it altogether, and apply all skills simultaneously, thereby giving, from the earliest stages, the appearance of depth and adequacy that is so pleasing in a "traditional" or as the reviewer states "classical" orientation to English teaching.

The existence of a hierarchy of skills can be easily perceived, for example, when it is realized that if one wishes to teach the skill named on the left of the series below, then one needs to have developed in the learner some competence in the skills named adjacent to it on the right.

1. Punctuation   Construction of simple statement sentences, question sentences, negative sentences.

2. Passive voice usage	Active-voice uses of the verb, tense inflections and participle inflections
3. Direct and Indirect Speech	All of (1) and (2) both left and right
4. Reporting	All of (1), (2) and (3)
5. Vocabulary	Most of (1) and (2) (development and expansion)
6. Summarizing	Most of (1) to (5)
7. Figures of speech, moods, themes in the literary analysis	Most of (1) to (6)
8. Advertisement analysis	Most of (1) to (6)

The main point is that if the learner is competent in the right-hand side of (1) and (2), then several of (3) to (8) can be tackled almost, though not completely, simultaneously. If, on the other hand, the learner is a Creole-speaking or Creole-influenced child, then the skills cannot be significantly and explicitly tackled; although it is conceded that some very informal and implicit acquisition of (3) to (8) will occur during the proper teaching of the right-hand side of (1) and (2). But to insist that during the first two years of a five-year programme of work with a second-dialect orientation, all of (1) to (8) must be present in the work of the first-year and extended in each of the subsequent years, is an abdication of responsibility for the tuition of the second-dialect learner.

One might wonder how and why it is possible that after more than three decades of awareness of the nature of the English-official Caribbean language situation, native-language approaches to English teaching such as one just illustrated, still hold so much sway. The question needs to be asked all the more because over the last two of the mentioned decades some progress has been made in Jamaica and the English-official Caribbean generally to develop a more rationally justifiable approach to the teaching of the Language Arts. For example, since the mid-1960s several publications of the present writer have outlined the second-dialect theory and practical procedures which are most relevant in the local situation (see Craig, 1966, 1967, 1969a, 1969b, 1973, 1980, 1983). The ideas in the latter work have been taken up and applied in a wide range of school materials. These include the *Lady Bird, Sunstart Reading Series* (publisher: Longman), which over many years has been the best-selling series of its kind;[2] the introductory books of the *New Caribbean* Readers (published: Ginn); the *Timehri Readers of Guyana*, and the *Primary Language Arts series*, produced in its final stages by Don Wilson and others starting from the already mentioned ideas of the present writer. The last mentioned series is issued free to primary schools by the Jamaican Ministry of Education, but there is no evidence that the principles which govern its con-struction have ever been seriously considered by more than a small handful of educators. Neither is there any indication of a will to extend those principles, as extended they can be, into the language education of the large masses of under-achievers in the use of English at the secondary level.

The main reason for the continuing dominance of native-language approaches to English teaching is to be found in the previous education of the majority of persons who are responsible for the training and school supervision in the Lan-guage Arts and English teaching. That education, like that of the writer, was one in which a university degree in English meant and still means English Literature. The recipients of that education, when faced with the strange task of teaching English language in schools, usually do one of two things. They may try to avoid it by packing the timetable with more fun-giving and pleasant replacements: impromptu drama, short stories and poems in Caribbean English (the novels are too long!), advertisement analysis, and so on. On the other hand they may revert to what they remember of language teaching from their own school days: the learning of grammatical facts about parts of speech and sentence structure, and whenever the teacher's time permits, exercises in writing where the same mistakes will always be made by the writers and underscored by the teacher.

For such a university graduate in English, postgraduate training to teach could be of help, depending on the specific orientation of that training. The odds at the moment are that the university graduate will aim to teach only in the high schools and will opt heavily for courses in the teaching of literature; after all, of the English syllabuses of the CXC, one is completely literature-focused and the other is at least half so, so why worry about language? A one-fourth interest in its teaching and a three-fourths interest in the teaching of litera-ture is all that is needed for the most prestigious of English-teaching positions. Apart from this, the majority chances are that the English tutor of the post-graduate student will have a literature orientation rather than a language one, and the student's interests will tend to be channelled accordingly. What helps to perpetuate this situation is that the university graduate, because of tradition, adverse conditions of work, and so on, will not be going to teach where the major language problem is: in the primary, all-age and new secondary schools. Therefore the principle of relevance dictates in any case that students and tutor should concentrate on the major locus of employment for graduates: the pres-tigious high schools.

If university graduates and their tutors in educational training had an ade-quate linguistic orientation, perceptions would undoubtedly be different and the results of training would be different too; but linguistics is young as a discipline, and in addition to this, it has a reputation of being more difficult than literature. The result is predictable: very few graduates with linguistics come up for training as teachers of English in the English-official Caribbean.

But the university graduate, trained or untrained, is not the only teacher of English. What of the hundreds of teachers that are entering the educational system each year from the teachers' colleges? And these are the teachers on whom the major weight of the English-language teaching problem continues to fall. Most of these teachers leave college with some understanding of the Creole-language or 'dialect' situation and the need to teach the 'patterns and structures' of English; but in the same way as for *graduates* from the university, their expertise in and understanding of such teaching varies as widely as the multiplicity of educational orientations that their tutors might have.

There are still teacher-college tutors as there are university teachers and education officers who will tell you with pride, and in condemnation of second-language or second-dialect methods, which as far as they are concerned are boring 'drill methods', that what they believe in and what they teach to their students is something like 'the Hayakawa approach' to English teaching. It is instructive, therefore, to look for a moment at this approach, and to see what it means for the vast majority of Creole-speaking or Creole-influenced children. The approach is well exemplified in the following statement:

> What is the teacher's first duty when a child says in class, "Taters ain't doin' good this year"? Traditionally, teachers of English and speech have seen their first duty as that of correcting the child's grammar, pronunciation, and diction in order to bring these up to literate standards. Teachers with a semantic orientation will give priority to a different task. They will ask the student such questions as "What potatoes do you mean? Those on your parents' farm or those throughout the country? From personal observations? From reports from credible sources?" In short, teachers of semantics will concern themselves, and teach their students to concern themselves, first of all with the truth, the adequacy, and the degree of trustworthiness of statements. (Hayakawa, 1939: vii)

Now no sensible person will attempt to quarrel with Hayakawa, that attention to fullness of information, precision, and clear and logical thinking are of the utmost importance in the use of language; but the overriding question is: which language? Is the society totally unaware of non-standard speech and writing? If it is, then the society should be consistent, and teachers in following the Hayakawa approach should be made to use the same non-standard language that they consider adequate for the child. If the society is not unaware, then, to say the least, it is illogical and irresponsible to expect that children who spend most of their days and nights in non-standard speech contexts will purely incidentally acquire standard speech, as the Hayakawa quotation suggests.

It should be noted, however, that the point about the Hayakawa quotation and the method it supports is not that they are attempting to say anything about teaching *new language;* what they are attempting to do, and doing very efficiently, is saying something about the development of communication strategies and the capacity for critical thinking in any *language and irrespective of language.* If those who talk about the "Hayakawa method" understand this, then they would not directly nor indirectly continue to shirk their responsibility to teach a standard language. What they would do is teach a standard language as efficiently as possible, while at the same time ensuring the development of thinking that Hayakawa was aiming at.

But let us return to that increasing number of teachers and teacher-educators who believe that English, as a new language to the child, must in some way be explicitly taught in the schools. Many of those who are well-intentioned in this respect still often fail to put into practice the cardinal principle that learning new language is learning new habits of performance rather than new facts about language. An example will clarify what is meant. In syllabuses and schemes of work in English, at both primary and secondary levels, the following item seems almost certain to appear: subject-verb accord. And if the teaching of the item is observed in classrooms from Kingston through to Port of Spain and on to Georgetown, the observer is likely to find that in a majority of cases, teachers will attempt to 'teach' it in one or two sessions, with wrong information, such as: "a singular subject must have a singular verb" and "the verb, unlike the noun, takes an *s* when it is singular, and nothing when it is plural."

They thereby confuse the children by ignoring *i* and *you* as subjects, and by ignoring tenses where the verb does not change to express number. The better teachers on the other hand will not make such mistakes. With both sets of teachers, however, the prevailing methodology to be observed is likely to be one whereby the children are made to understand or learn the facts or rules about subject-verb concord, and then to apply those rules by doing multiple choice, filling-in-the-blanks, or other examination types of questions.

It is still relatively rare to see a teacher interpret the topic, subject-verb concord, as necessitating, not testing activities in one or two sessions, but sustained and creative practice in sentence making, using the parts of the verbs *be, do, and have,* and the present simple tense of all other verbs. The point is that the full implications of the fact that, in second-dialect as in foreign-language teaching, language has to be taught and learned as a habit has not yet firmly taken hold.

There are several reasons why this is so, but we might mention only the two most important ones. Firstly, teachers point to the pressure of examinations and the forms of examination questions, from the Common entrance to the CXC Examination. These examinations dominate the curriculum, starting from the primary school. This is not the fault of the examinations, however, but the fault of those who teach and who forget the difference between teaching and testing. Many teachers are continuously testing their children, often with constant doses of multiple-choice questions, with the result that very little is really taught to the children, very little is learned.

Secondly, teaching for habit-formation in English, rather than for the learning of facts about English goes against a massive weight of traditional practices which resist innovation and change. The more senior persons in the education system, when given opportunities for further training, are usually given those opportunities in the area of administration, management and supervision, seldom in the areas of greater depth in curriculum content and in new, innovative and more relevant classroom methodologies and materials. The result is that especially in a field like English teaching in second-dialect situations, where the most significant developments are relatively recent, there tend to be differences between the knowledge and understandings of those who are recently trained and consequently relatively junior in the education system, and those who are now in management and supervisory positions, but with an earlier training that gave a different orientation in curriculum and teaching strategies. This writer has experienced the constant complaints of young teachers who come for certificate diploma training at the university. They point out, for example, that innovative strategies which would give children more intensive practice speaking and writing English, require less marking of errors by the teacher, get children to read more both in and out of the classroom, save wastage of classroom time and effort by getting children to develop skills in a hierarchy rather than simultaneously, are actively hampered, if not made completely impossible. Factors indicated as restrictive of these strategies are the customary form of the school timetable, the rules of the school in matter relating to tests and their content, the beliefs and expectations of more senior teachers, as well as of education officers, and the expectations of parents.

In this situation, what are the prospects for the future? It would seem that at both the primary and secondary levels, pressures are mounting and will continue to mount for improved efficiency in the teaching of the Language Arts and

English. Those sectors of the region that need to communicate locally as well as internationally in a standard language are already voicing increasing impatience with a teaching profession that allows illiteracy and Creole monolingualism to be inevitable for a majority of school leavers. What is holding back the censure of teachers at the moment is the undoubtedly poor conditions under which they are known to work in many primary, all-age, and new secondary schools. But the improvement that is necessary in teaching is much greater than what can be expected to match desired improvements in physical and material conditions. The quality and quantity of the product from each teacher will need to be greater.

With education becoming progressively more egalitarian, even the more prestigious high schools will feel the increasing impact, as they are in fact already doing, of Creole language influences in their populations, and the absence of home experiences in reading among the children of the poor. In this context, those teachers and teacher educators who find it still possible to take English, as a linguistic system, for granted will have to find more explicit ways of teaching it; so that the learning of it as structure, system and habit will proceed concurrently with the growth of the intellect and emotions through its use.

Notes

1. A first version of this paper was prepared for the seminar "On the Removal of Language Barriers", UNESCO and the Jamaican Ministry of Education, Kingston, Jamaica, January, 1987. Modifications have been made to the original so as to provide relevance in the present paper to the English-official Caribbean in general.
2. Although this series acknowledges its indebtedness to the writer's ideas, the writer has not in any way been financially involved in the series.

References

Acheson, K.H., and M.D. Gall. 1980. *Techniques in Clinical Supervision of Teachers*. New York: Longman.

Advocate News. 1976. Barbados, 1 July 1976.

Aiken, L.R. 1973. "Ability and creativity in mathematics". SIMEAC, Eric Information Centre, Ohio State University, Columbia, Ohio.

Allen, E.L. 1966. "New deal for education in independent Jamaica". *Ministry Paper No. 73*. Ministry of Education, Jamaica.

———. 1965–66. "Note to Cabinet on education policy". Mimeo. Jamaica.

Archer, B. 1978. "Time for a revolution in art and design education". *Royal College of Art Papers,* No. 6. London.

Asher, J.J. 1977. *Learning Another Language Through Actions: The Complete Teacher's Guide.* Los Gatos, CA: Sky Oaks Production.

Bacchus, K. 1969. "Education and decolonization". *New World Quarterly* 5 (1 & 2). Trinidad.

Bacchus, K., and C. Brock (eds). 1987. "The challenge of scale: educational development in the small states of the Commonwealth". Commonwealth Secretariat, London.

Bailey, B. 1963. "Teaching of English noun-verb concord in primary schools in Jamaica". *Caribbean Quarterly* 9 (4).

———. 1966. *Jamaican Creole Syntax.* Cambridge: Cambridge University Press.

Banks, L.J. 1973. "Curriculum developments in Britain 1961–8". In R. Hooper (ed.), *The Curriculum: Context, Design and Development.* Edinburgh: Oliver & Boyd/ Open University Press.

Becher, T., and S. Maclure. 1978. *The Politics of Curriculum Change.* London: Hutchinson.

Beddoe, I.B. 1976. "Social studies and the Social Studies Project UWI, St Augustine". *Social Studies Education* 6: 14–15.

———. 1981a. "On-going research in moral education". *Social Studies Education* 18: 43.

Cassidy, F. 1961. *Jamaica Talk.* New York: Macmillan.

Craig, D.R. 1966. "Teaching English to Jamaican Creole speakers: A model of multi-dialect situation". *Language Learning* 16 (1–2).

———. 1967. "Some early indications of learning a second dialect". *Language Learning* 17 (3–4).

———. 1969a. "Teaching language and literacy for language learning". In A. Aarons, B. Gordon and W. Stewart (eds.), *Linguistic-cultural Differences in American Education.* Special Anthology Issue. *Florida Foreign Language Reporter* (Spring–Summer).

———. 1969b. "Bidialectal education: Creole and Standard in the West Indies". In *Review of Applied Linguistics in Language Teaching.* Exeter: University of Exeter, Publications Clerk.

———. 1973. "Social class, language and communication in Jamaican children". In *Education in the Commonwealth* 6. London: Commonwealth Secretariat.

———. 1980. "A Creole English Continuum and the Theory of Grammar". In *Varieties of English around the World*, edited by R.R. Day, vol. 2. Heidelberg: Julius Groos Verlag.

———. 1983. "Teaching Standard English to non-Standard speakers: Some methodological issues". *Journal of Negro Education* 52: 65–74.

Hayakawa. 1939. *Language in Thought and Action.* New York: Harcourt.

Le Page, R. 1957–58. "General outlines of Creole English in the British Caribbean". *Orbis* 6: 373–91; 7: 54–64.

Le Page, R. and D. DeCamp. 1960. "Jamaican Creole". *Creole Language Studies* 1, pt. 2. New York: Macmillan.

Walters, E. 1957. "Learning to read in Jamaica". Mona, Jamaica, UWI, Department of Education.

7 | A Creole English Continuum and the Theory of Grammar

Abstract

Previous studies of continuum situations have adopted grammatical formulations that are incapable of representing the linguistic knowledge of speakers in such situations. What is required is a grammar that is capable of representing the invariant conceptual element that can underlie syntactic and lexical variation, and that is capable of showing the relationships between variant syntactic and lexical forms. Some proposals are made towards such a grammar and some implications are discussed in relation to studies of variation and studies of socially determined differenced in the use of language.

Introduction

If it comes to making a tentative theoretical stand most of us would probably say, like Labov (1973, p. 43): "We will adhere for the present to the Chomskyan notion that the grammar might represent the knowledge that the native speaker needs to produce and understand the language in native fashion"; and (1971, p. 465): "... we can use Chomsky's insights and profit tremendously from generative grammar, but not if we allow him to define for us the limits of linguistics and the shape of linguistic rules . . .". What is surprising is that after this vigilant and selective acceptance, most of us proceed, contradictorily, to accept without question the most fundamental and at the same time the most limiting of Chomsky's (1957, 1965) proposals, namely, that a grammar begins with a base component of the specific kind suggested by Chomsky.

Bickerton (1973) for example, referring to some of the most striking additions to sociolinguistic knowledge, makes proposals for polylectal grammars; in form, such grammars are shown as having a Chomskyan base component, except for a difficult-to-justify peculiarity (partly derived from Ross 1969) which allows 'be' as a higher predicate with its complement as a lower predicate, although there is the simultaneous, and apparently contradictory suggestion that the copula does not exist in deep structure; where the grammar departs from a standard generative model is really at the level of morphophonemics, a relatively superficial level, where "spelling rules" are permitted and combined in a "rule shift" component that would account for lectal variation.

The impression is given that what we have learned about continuum speech communities: the simultaneous processing by the speaker of overlapping systems of syntax and lexis, implicational hierarchies, intra-idiolectal variation, and so on offer no new possibilities for more explanatory descriptions of the form-meaning structure of language, except at a level of description where fundamental linguistic relationships and necessary inferences about the underlying knowledge of the speaker have already been established, and all that is left to be done is the listing and ordering of the superficial markers of such relationships and knowledge. In this respect, the latter impression is probably observable in the comment of Fraser (1973: 11) that:

> . . . variable rules describe the observable language behavior but do not explain this behavior in any sense of the word 'explain' . . . to stop with variable rules is to be satisfied with data collection and not explanation, much the same as demographic information describes but doesn't provide an explanation.

One gets the impression that although only variable rules are mentioned, the comment might also refer to implicational scales and those portions of polylectal grammars that are particularly polylectal.

It is to be noted, however, that Fraser's example of how formulations such as the latter might be given greater explanatory adequacy merely involves relating them to the general syntagtactics and phonotactics of language conceived as a static system. The possibility does not seem to be envisaged that facts relevant to variation and continuum situations might themselves justify changes in our conception of the more general or abstract grammar of language, and that it might not be wise at this stage of our knowledge to assume that variation has implications only for the ends of generative grammars.

It is to the discussion of the latter possibility that this paper seeks to make a contribution. The specific question: what does a language continuum, as such, have to suggest about the structure of the native speaker's linguistic knowledge, and about how this structure might be represented in a grammar?

Non-Existence, Deletion and Variable Representation

In an interview with Peter Roberts[1] who would normally be regarded as a teacher (– the children referred to him as "Sir"), two Jamaican 12-year olds, of urban low-socioeconomic status, answered the question: "What you would like to be when you leave school?" They replied:

(1) ai waan tiicha / tiichca / sor   12/1/A
     (I want (to be/turn a) teacher, sir

(2) ai waan nors.   12/1/A
     (I want (to be/turn a) nurse)

After further conversation, the interviewer went away, and the first child, talking to her peer (with whom she was then completely alone except for a third child and a concealed tape recorder) remarked:

(3) enihou ai di hier di siem taim di-man-dat
     (Anyhow I heard the same time that man

     taak bout se dat wi na-a torn nors/
     (talk about, – say that we'll not turn nurse (s)

     aid sie no chilron in sevn-yu kyanot
     (I'd say no children in 7U cannot

     torn nors / biko –
     (turn nurse(s), because –
     (And the third child interjected at this point)

(4)   wat dem gain tek *torn* it?
      (What are they going to to take and *turn* it? (i.e.
      What are they going to do in order to *turn* nurses?)   12/1B

The presence of /ai (instead of /mi/ , /aid/, /sie/ (instead of /se/) and other indications mark this language as mesolectal to some extent. These children would however experience no problem in conversing with a basilectal Jamaican Creole (JC) speaker, whatever the basilect is, and no problem either, except for unfamiliar lexis, if such occurs, in conversing with a Standard English (SE) speaker. It may be said that these children can operate quite comfortably in the Jamaican speech continuum and respond to any speaker, so long as they themselves are left free to produce their own brand of preferred language.

What is significant for us at the moment is the similarity of the VP's in 1 and 2, and the difference between the latter and the VP's italicized in 3 and 4. It is to be noted that 3 is produced by the speaker of 1 who, in the first instance used the same VP construction as the speaker of 2, but who subsequently reinterpreted the statement of the speaker of 2 and supplied the item:

(5)   / . . torn . . . /
      (to turn a . . .)

which was originally absent in both 1 and 2.

One might ask the reason for the realization of /torn/ in 3, and its non-realization in 1 and 2. One answer might be that the speaker of 3 had no choice at all to do otherwise. 'Become' which is synonymous in this case with 'turn' is not in the basilectal repertoire of JC and is rare even in the mesolect, and there was no item like /waan/ in 1 and 2 that could render the surface realization of / torn/ unnecessary. But one can still ask why /torn/ can be assumed to be unnecessary in 1 and 2; it is to be noticed that the item is strictly obligatory in the SE gloss. The answer lies in the fact that in JC, there is a rule which states as follows:

(6)   Nouns that denote persons by occupation (which will here be taken as being in a general category of 'function-defined' nouns) become abstract nouns, denoting occupation itself when the meaning of the verbs requires it.

The fact that this rule exists in JC is independently attested by the fact that function-defined nouns can often be found as direct objects of verb which leave no possibility at all that the person rather than the occupation could be intended. Witness for example:

(7)   Shi lorn tu duu *taipis*   12/25/A
      (She learnØ to do *typist*.)
      i.e. "She learned typing."

It is therefore clearly evident that so far as the speakers here relevant are concerned, the VP's in 1 and 2 could simultaneously have two surface-level representations in the acrolect, as shown in 8 and 9. Indeed, there is a third possible representation, 10, which is ruled out only because of the discourse context.

(8)   ... want (to do) teaching/nursing

(9)   ... want (to be/turn a) teacher/nurse

(10)   ... want a teacher/nurse

But the behaviour of the speakers gives no indication whatsoever that the deep structural representation, i.e. the meanings, of the VP's at 8 and 9 are similarly ambivalent. Nevertheless, the speakers themselves shift between the different surface-level representations; one shift is seen when the speaker of 1 produces /torn/ in 3; and another shift of an even more complex kind is probably seen when the third child, interrupting the speaker of 3, produces 4. The latter sentence, although copying the verb /torn/ which requires the person rather than the occupation complement, yet contains the *tek + NP* construction that would have the SE meaning:

(11)   With what will they turn it?

Where *tek+NP* is the nominal JC representation of the SE instrument phrase. Person and occupation together here seem to take on a combined significance.

To describe the linguistic knowledge of speakers who will produce 1, 2, 3 and 4 in the same discourse and at the same time understand their SE equivalents, a grammar that can do the following things is needed.

(12)   (a) For a given sentence, like 2, the grammar must be able to specify
            the actual conceptual elements or meanings contained in 2.

(b) It must be able to show that the conceptual elements contained in 2 are the same as those contained in 8 and 9.

(c) It must be able to show the relationship between the syntactic form of 2, and those of 8 and 9.

There are, in addition, other things that the grammar would need to be able to do, like specifying the determinants of the selection of one surface form rather than another. We should note, however, that in so far as references to deep structure and surface structure in the required grammar are concerned, there is the question of whether there is a formally distinguishable level of deep structure. Such a question might be regarded as pointless, as discussed for example in Lakoff and Ross (1967), McCawley (1968), and Chomsky (1972), and as one that might better be assigned, according to Bedell (1974), to a controversy about grammatical notation and terminology. 'Deep structure' is what the theorist uses in order to describe the knowledge which a speaker must have before producing a meaningful linguistic output or for that speaker to comprehend such an output. It is only problematic when one tries to restrict this conception to somebody's prejudices in order to make a specific theoretical formulation.

If a grammar can provide the specifications suggested in 12, it might account incidentally for some paraphrase relationships of the kind stated in Chomsky (1965) as being unaccounted for in grammatical models at that time, and that still remain unaccounted for after the passing of the 1970s. It is not yet clear whether such a grammar might unjustifiably be committed to the Indo-European camp, as Bickerton (1973: 22) did with regard to Creoles, although it is to be noted that in the particular continuum under discussion here, the unified and smoothly integrated movement of individuals between basilect and acrolect means that the individual has an implicit and very active knowledge of the correspondence between whatever is in his basilect and whatever is its representation in the Indo-European camp. The possibility is that the latter and all other possible camps might be closely unified in terms of the knowledge of any speaker.

The Minimal SVO Sentence

In the search for a grammar that might be able to do the things just stated, certain characteristics of the continuum that seem to have a bearing on base-level sentence structure ought possibly to be investigated. The present discussion can examine only one set of these characteristics: some alternative forms of the SVO sentence, but it is hoped that this will provide a direction for further investigation.

In JC (cf. Bailey, 1966), there is a passive voice which is not separately marked morphologically so as to be distinguished from the active, and there is no 'by'-passive phrase. Bailey (1966: 81) does not refer to it as a passive voice at all, but regards it as resulting from an optional transformation by which the direct object becomes subject as a preliminary to the verb becoming adjectivalized. However, since there is a structure with which it might be compared at the opposite pole of the continuum, we will here retain the term 'passive voice'. Examples are as follows:

(13)   it tek out   12/5/B
       (It has been taken out)

(14)   shi . . . . . get chruu wan shaat-kot we sel fish   12/12/B
       (She . . . . got through a short-cut where fish is sold)

(15)   shi mus gyet biit   12/28/A
       (She must be beaten)

One might ask how the basilectal speaker/hearer distinguishes between active and passive. The answer is that he/she makes that distinction solely by the presence or absence of direct objects and by the animateness restrictions that are obligatory in the subjects or objects of transitive verbs. Thus, a passive voice interpretation is obligatory for (13) because no direct object is present. In (14), the antecedent of /we/ is shaat-kot/ which can be regarded as the subject of /sel/; this means that the subject being not only *-animate* but also impossible as agent of /sel/, and the direct object /fish/ being present in the sentence, it becomes obligatory to interpret the verb as being in the passive voice, since an active-voice interpretation is nonsensical in that context.

By similar conventions, a sentence such as:

(16)   Bari lik ; (lik = 'hit')

would be difficult to interpret in JC, because it could be active or passive unless there was some elucidatory context. Nevertheless it might still receive some interpretation because some exclusion of unlikely meanings is still possible.

If the sentence was intended to mean "Barry hits" (i.e. habitually or usually), it would most likely be:

(17)   Bari lik piipl
       (Barry hits people)

and if a passive-voice meaning was intended, the sentence could possibly, though not obligatorily be:

(18)   *Either* (a) Bari get lik
       (Barry was hit. Literally: Barry got hit)
       Or (b) dem lik Bari
       (Barry was hit: Literally: They hit Barry)

However, if the subject of 16 was changed so as to give a sentence like this one:

(19)   di guot lik
       (the goat was hit)

It is practically certain that the sentence would receive an immediate passive-voice interpretation, without any context being necessary, since the nature of the subject 'goat' and its animateness status makes such an interpretation practically obligatory.

These facts about the JC passive concern *activity* as distinct from *stative* verbs. In the former (i.e. activity) verbs, what seems very important, and what seems to underlie the speaker's reliance on animateness restrictions and the presence or absence of likely subjects and direct objects, is the concept 'do' in its activity as distant from its auxiliary-verb sense. This activity 'do' concept seems very strong in the relevant verbs as the well-known SE restriction seen in 20 and 21 shows:

(20)   What Barry did was hit the goat

(21)   *What Barry did was lick the goat

In the examples the activity 'do' concept, which is focused upon, is present in (20) but not in (21), hence the respective well-formedness in one case and deviance in the other. It could be said then that in JC the interpretation of a passive voice is possible only if the subject of the verb is incompatible, for one reason or another, with the inherent activity- -'do' concept of the relevant transitive verb.

From these facts, it seems possible to describe the meaning of an activity, SVO, sentence such as

(22)   Bari lik di guot
       (Barry hit the goat)

as consisting of two separate components. The first component would consist of an NP linked to the activity- 'do' concept and the second component would consist of another NP linked to a concept or a set of concepts that is stative in its meaning (as a passive-voice verb is) and that embodies the result of the activity in the first component. The linkage between the two components, in order to embody the meaning that the activity in the first component is 'causal' or directed toward achieving the state in the second, needs to be more than just coordinate linkage. It suggested therefore that the linkage between the two components is of the same kind as that indicated sometimes by the complementizer 'that' when it follows the deictic or rudimentary manner-adverb 'so' in natural language. The components may be diagrammed as in (23), where stative-VP can possibly be a complex of coordinately-linked stative VP's in the form: *stative-VP and VP and VP . . .*:

(23) $(NP_1$ activity- 'do so' $(NP_2$ stative-VP))

Since the level of the representation of (23) is a conceptual one, it seems best at the moment that the concepts be labelled as shown, to avoid misunderstandings.

The deep structure shown in (23) can provide a derivation for varied surface-level results depending on whether the speaker has the deep-level intention of topicalizing NP_1 or NP_2. Topicalization (TOP) is here conceived as an 'intention', similar in its grammatical status to Q , Imp and other indicators of the speaker's purpose commonly used in current grammatical models. It is conceived that an ordered set of topicalizations is, at least in SE, possible within the same sentence. Possibly, one deep-level difference between JC and SE is that JC does not allow secondary topicalization as shown in (24c) below, while SE does. The conception of the role of topicalization here suggested is not incompatible with that stated in Fillmore (1968, 4.4) for example, although the conclusions about the necessary form of a grammar are different. The surface results of the varied placing of topicalizations on the elements in (23), using the lexical content of (22), are shown in (24).

(24)

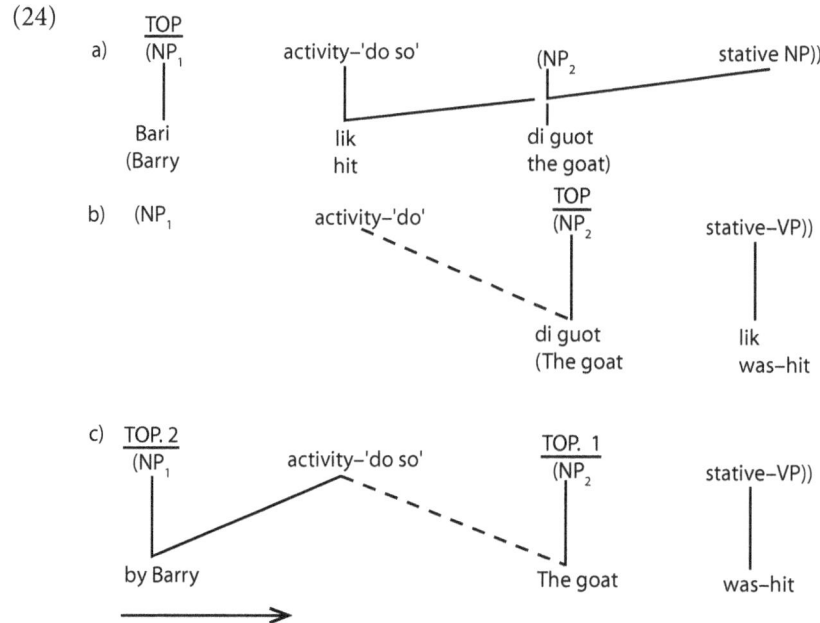

It is well known, although it is generally ignored in current grammatical models, that the active and passive voice forms of the apparently same sentence do not have exactly the same meaning. The difference in meanings lies in the topicalization intent of the speaker as here suggested. It is further suggested that the varied placing of topicalization on the verb elements in the conceptual, base sentoids, as well as the possibilities for all types of topicalization to be affected by the specific context of sentences, would result in some of the different forms of 'split' sentence that are well known. Inherent in these proposals is the suggestion that increased explanatory adequacy in a grammar requires that a single base-level representation must be capable of giving rise to a variety of surface derivations in such a way that each separate surface result might be shown to originate in some specific motivation, like topicalization or focus or question for example, of the speaker.

One might ask how the proposal in (24) would apply in the case of stative, transitive verbs, from which the activity-'do so' concept is obviously missing, as illustrated in 21). It is very significant that the JC basilect allows no passivization of stative verbs. For example:

(25)   They liked Barry

(26)   Barry was liked (b y them).

(27)   /dem laik Bari/.

(28)   */Bari laik/; * /Bari get laik/

(29)   They liked the ice cream

(30)   The ice cream was liked (by them).

(31)   dem laik di ais kriim

(32)   */di ais kriim laik/

where, although (25) and (27) in one instance and (29) and (31) in the other are parallel acceptable sentences at opposite extremes of the continuum, their passivizations (26/28) and (30/32) respectively are not. Because of this, it would not be justifiable to suggest a deep structure approximately to (24) for stative, transitive verbs; that this should be so is not surprising because surface differences of the kind relevant here between stative verbs and other verbs ought to have deep structural origins or consequences (whichever term is preferred); to indicate the latter by the *device + stative* is probably description, but certainly not explanation. The required deep structure would need to reflect the fact that a stative, transitive verb generally represents some affective or sensory characteristic of its subject, and the relationship of subject-NP to object-NP is generally no more than that the latter is in existence as the topic of the sensory or affective characteristics of the former. These facts may possibly be captured within the format of the two-sentoid configuration used in 23), and illustrated as in (33) using the lexical content of (29).

(33)   a)

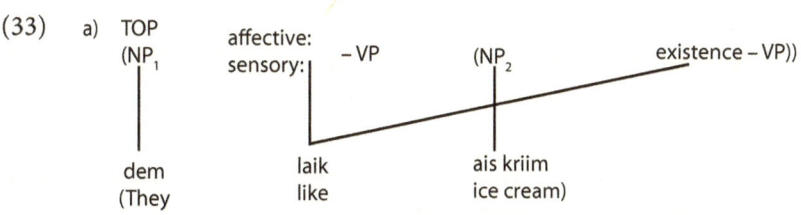

b)   *JC procedure with topicality on NP₂*

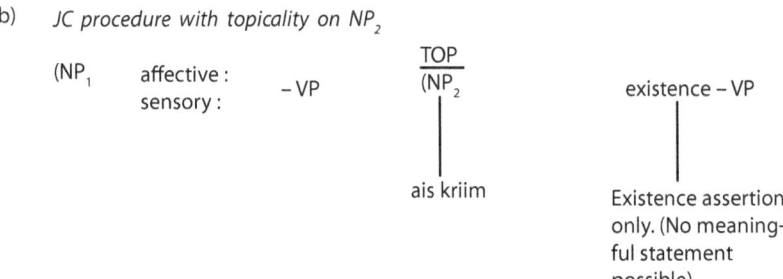

c)   *SE procedure with topicality on NP₂*

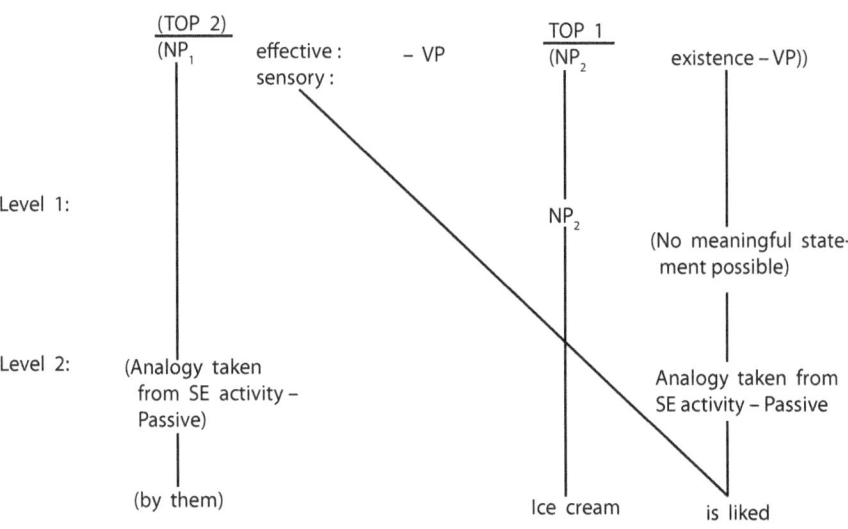

The illustration is intended to suggest that the sentence in (33 a) can occur at both ends of the continuum, but that the basilectal speaker, if he/she seeks to topicalize NP_2, as shown in (33b) will find a blockage because the deep level VP that is related to NP_2, gives no possibility of a meaningful statement; the basilectal speaker will be forced to choose some other communication alternative. The acrolectal speaker, on the other hand, finding the same blockage, is permitted by the conventions of his language to take an analogy from the format of the activity-Passive, as shown in (33c), with the result that a passivization of the affective/sensory-VP of the first sentoid takes place. It is possible that the acrolect allows this freedom to choose a structural analogy merely because it possesses a greater quantity of near-surface structural devices, while the basilect, on the other hand, cannot do the same because its surface structures remain closer in form to the general conceptual base underlying language.

Many other facts about transitive and intransitive-verb behaviour at polar extremes of the continuum seem explainable within this framework. For example, Fillmore (1968: 4) mentions the difficulty of explaining the deviance in (37).

(34)   John ruined the table

(35)   John built the table

(36)   What John did to the table was ruin it.

(37)   * What John did to the table was build it.

Apart from the pragmatic reality mentioned by Fillmore that whether the object existed before or after the action has something to do with the deviance, there is also the related fact of the conceptual difference between 'do' and 'do to'; the former represents a link between the subject and the verb, and can apply irrespective of whether the object existed before the action; the latter, on the other hand, represents a link between the activity – 'do so' concept and the object itself, and needs the prior existence of the object before it can be realized. This fact is diagrammed in (24 b) and (24 c) by the broken line which links the activity 'do so' concept of the first sentoid to the NP of the second sentoid. This link would of necessity be absent conceptually in verbs like 'build', and it would also be absent conceptually in verbs like 'like', as is suggested in the diagrams at (33). An extension of this single explanation takes care of another kind of transitive-verb behaviour that does not seem adequately explainable in current grammatical models: this is the difference in meaning between different forms of those transitive verbs (otherwise, causative verbs) whose direct objects can become subjects of the verbs with or without passivization as in (38, 39, 40). In basilect JC, all three of the latter sentences would be expressed as in (41).

(38)   The stick broke

(39)   The stick was broken (i.e. it is known that someone broke the stick)

(40)   The stick was broken (i.e. the stick was found in a broken state)

(41)   JC: /di stik brok/.

The relevant extension of the explanation is as follows: For (38), the speaker entertains no activity – 'do so' concept at all and 'broke' is practically stative in its meaning. If it is to be diagrammed, it would need to be shown as having the same form as the right-hand (or second) sentoid of (23), standing alone without a first sentoid; but in its context (i.e. discourse context), there would need to be some indication that someone witnessed the 'breaking'. The deep structure of (40) would be similar, except that the discourse context would have to exclude a witness. Example (39) however, would have a deep structure similar to (24 b), necessitating two sentoids with the NP of the first being indefinite and with a link between the activity – 'do so' and 'stick'. So far as (41), the JC surface representation is concerned, the deep structures would vary in the same way as just explained, although the surface form would remain invariable. It might be additionally pointed out that the explanation here given of (39) and (40) applies not just to 'causative' verbs of the 'break/burn/roll' variety, but to the passive forms of all transitive verbs which permit a similar ambiguity (e.g. "The door was shut") not so far adequately explained in current grammatical models. Although Hasegawa (1968) takes them into account in his treatment of the passive which involves also a complementized second sentoid at a base level, he does so without any splitting into component concepts as is suggested here.

The preceding proposals can easily accommodate an account of the instrument phrase that is optional with transitive verbs. In this respect, it is very significant that in the JC basilect, the acrolectal 'with' + Instrument NP is most often expressed as /tek/ + NP as in (42).

(42)   shi tek tamrin wip an biit di children   12/28/A
        (She took a tamarind whip and beat the children
        i.e. She beat the children with a tamarind whip)

It is not at all unlikely that this basilectal form should represent the deep structural origin of the instrument phrase, which at a surface level in the acrolect would become represented as a preposition-phrase; and in grammatical terms, it would mean no more than the addition of a single sentoid to the two that would normally represent a single SVO sentence without the instrument phrase. The deep structure of (42) may be diagrammed as in (43) for example.

(43)

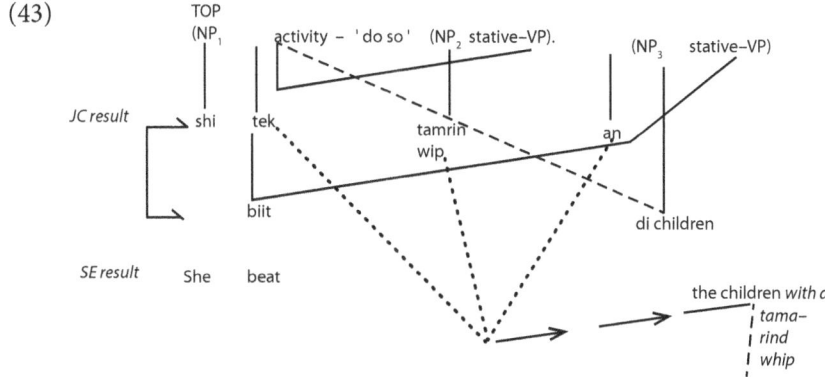

It seems deserving of more than a passing note that both agentive 'by' and instrumental-'with', the preposition phrases that obligatorily need to be taken into account in the grammar of the transitive verb, have been reduced within the present proposals to a common origin in deep-level sentoids. Without further discussing the question at this time, the strongly intuitive difference between the latter propositions (i.e. 'by' and 'with') and other prepositions can therefore be accounted for. It will also be noted that the well-known possibilities of the instrument NP taking on the role of subject are well accommodated within the present proposals, since the sentoids containing the instrumental and object NP's can combine to produce an SVO sentence having the form of (23) except that the first sentoid would not in this case contain activity- 'do so'; the fact that activity- 'do so' would thus be absent however would be reflected in surface structure by the tendency towards deviance which is observable in (44b) when understood in conjunction with (44a) and (44c), taken from Fillmore (1968: 22). What Fillmore labels as case relationships is here discussed so as to show the conceptual constituents of such relationships.

(44)   (a) John broke the window with a hammer.
        (b) **What a hammer did was break the window.
        (c) A hammer broke the window.

One of the facts about a sentence like (44a) which does not seem to have been particularly noticed in previous treatments is the lack of communication in the sentence about what the subject NP (in this case 'John') really did. In purely pragmatic terms, he must have held the hammer and imparted force to it, but after that he might either have continued holding it or he might have thrown it. All that we know is that he must have done something or other (i.e., activity- 'do so'), and it was the hammer really (together with the window) that was really directly involved in the pragmatic result that we label 'broke'. In the present treatment, these pragmatic necessities, which after all must be the basis of conceptualization and language, seem to be correctly represented by the fact that it is in the sentoids of the instrumental and object NP's that the content of the verbs reside, and in the 'stative' form that a pragmatic result would necessarily be in; the 'active' principle, on the other hand, which needs to merge with the 'stative' one to produce the full meaning of a transitive verb, resides in the sentoid of the agent or subject.

The preceding proposals seem capable of providing a basis for describing the deep grammar of transitive, partially transitive and intransitive verbs according to the ways they function at both extremes of the continuum. In the case of the partially transitive and intransitive verbs, one necessary modification in the structural description would be that the NP in the second sentoid would be a repeat of the one in the first. However, there are a number of verbs of several different kinds that would need to be described by more complex extensions of the basic two-sentoid pattern so far suggested, but the scope of the present paper forbids a more detailed discussion. What has emerged so far in relation to the Creole-English continuum is as follows:

(45) (a) An explanation of the simultaneous processing of multiple surface-level representations of an invariant underlying meaning or concept requires that a grammatical base consisting of primitive conceptual elements, all selected from natural language, should first be postulated.

(b) The behaviour of the minimal SVO sentence in the Creole-English continuum suggests that stative verbals (including some classes of affective and secondary verbals), the concepts 'and', and 'do' and 'so', the 'that'-clause relationship between sentences, a number of *intentions* (Top, Q etc.) which speakers are known to express, the concept 'not' the concept NP (or in non-syntactic terms 'entity'), and the combination of *NP ('be')* verbal are some of the primitive conceptual elements in the grammatical base.

(c) Specific combinations of the conceptual elements of the grammatical base or, in other terms, segments of base sentences, can be lexically re-labelled so that the conceptual elements of the base remain as the ultimate meanings of the lexical terms.

Hypotheses towards a Grammar

The preceding conclusions, while suggesting the possibility of analyzing the internal conduct of verbals into component conceptual elements, have made no similar suggestion about nouns. In relation to nouns, the same possibility is implied, nevertheless, not only by what has so far been said here, but by the well-known fact that the selectional restrictions of nouns are themselves stative predicates, and that they create the practical effect of making nouns, in ordinary grammar, appear to be no more than a syntactic category symbol (in this case NP, a mere concept of 'entity' followed by certain defining predicates in the general form:

(46) NP (be-) count *and* (be-) animate *and* (be-) male *and* . . .
          mass inanimate female
          singular
          plural

Katz and Fodor, in their well-known formulations, suggested in effect that all the meanings of any given noun might be represented by the isolation of additional features, whether syntactic or semantic. The latter suggestion however has never become practicable, for the important reason, that as suggested in Bolinger (1965) for example, a potentially infinite number of features would need to be determined. On the surface, this fact would seem to militate as well against the present proposal. On further consideration, however, it becomes evident that the potential infinity of semantic features comes from the fact that the dictionary definition of the noun can interact with a potentially infinite number of semantic features within the noun. In short, the potential infinity lies in external contexts, and not in the internal features of the noun. This discussion, again, cannot be taken further on this occasion, but sufficient has been said to indicate the general directions of the present hypotheses, quite apart from the validity or invalidity any proposals of a different kind such as those in Bach (1968), for example.

Another area that needs some incidental clarification before the form of a grammar can be outlined is that which concerns the distinction between stative and active verbals. Schachter (1973), for example, questions the empirical basis of the distinction and suggests that the three criteria, acceptability of the imperative, the *do- something* contribution, and the progressive, by which the stative-active distinction is supposed to be determined, do not give consistent results with assumedly stative or active items. In support of this contention Schachter cites (47, 48 and 49):

(47)   a. Be here at six o'clock.
       b. What you'll do is be here at six o'clock.
       c. *You're being here at six o'clock.

(48)   a. *Miss the parade.
       b. What you'll do is miss the parade.
       c. You're missing the parade.

(49)   a. Remember to write.
       b. *Don't remember to write.
       c. Forget to write.
       d. Don't forget to write.

These examples, however, contrary to Schachter's suggestions, provide no evidence against the consistency of the stative-active distinction since in each case the critical lexical item in the starred sentence is semantically different from its counterpart in the unstarred sentences, although it shares a common phonological shape. In each case, what distinguishes a genuinely stative meaning of a given phonological shape from an active meaning cannot be regarded as referencing any behaviour that is within the voluntary control or subject to the will of the subject of the verbal. Schachter understood this and stated it in effect, but he did not consider shifts of meaning from one example to another.

With the use of conventional symbols so far as possible, the rules of the proposed grammatical base may now be outlined as follows:

(50)

$$S \rightarrow [\text{NP } \text{VP (S)}] \quad (\textit{and } S)$$

$$\text{NP} \rightarrow \begin{bmatrix} I \\ \textit{something} \\ S \end{bmatrix} \quad (\textit{and } \text{NP})$$

$$VP \rightarrow (not \left\{ (be) \left[\begin{array}{l} Adj \\ Pred.\ Adv. \\ Deictic \\ S \end{array} \right] \\ V\ [S] \right\} (and\ VP)$$

Adj. →   <u>Sensation</u>:   black, blue ... bitter, sweet ... good
             <u>Shape, size, number, quantity</u>: broad, deep ... big,
                     little ... more, less ... one, two ...
                     many, several ... first, second ... some,
                     all ...

Pred. Adv. →   <u>Location</u>: somewhere, everywhere ... in, on ...
                    belong ...
             <u>Time</u> :   now, then ...
     Deictic →   <u>Manner</u> : so
        V →   <u>Sensation</u>: feel, hear, see ... sound ...
              <u>Psychological</u>: afraid, angry, pleased ... hate,
                     like, want ... believe, know, think ...
                     mean ...
             <u>Activity</u> :   do (so)

Apart from being consistent with the conclusions earlier reached, the constituents of the proposed grammatical base reflect a certain fundamental relationship between language and human cognition which has never, so far, been
reflected in grammatical formulations, despite Chomsky's repeated assertions
to the effect that language is a part of human psychology. If the latter assertions
are true, then linguistic structure must in its fundamental aspects be parallel
to the structure of conceptualization, and must be based upon the details of
human sensory perceptions and human cognitive abilities. It seems extremely
significant that lexical labels for such perceptions and abilities are marked in a
special way by the *stative* characteristic, and it ought to be natural that those
lexical items and the relationships inherent in them (like the relationships of
NP VP, VP [S], and 'and') should represent the base of the human faculty of
language, as it here suggested.

A natural-language sentence represented in terms of the suggested base
would of necessity appear as an apparently cumbersome string of possibly
numerous two-part sentoids, but the cumbersomeness of this base string would
be of the same nature as that of the machine language of a computer as compared

with the elegance of a sophisticated programming language for the same computer; the computer would be incapable of functioning however unless the elegant programming language can be translated into the cumbersome machine language. From the given base, the grammar would operate by a succession of simultaneously lexical and syntactic re-labellings as aimed at in (45c). For this to happen all that is further necessary is a stratified lexicon in which

1. the meanings or conceptual content of items of the first stratum will be represented only in terms of base items,
2. the content of items of each stratum after the first will be represented primarily in terms of items from the immediately preceding stratum in conjunction, only to such an extent as is absolutely necessary, with items from any farther-removed, preceding stratum, including the base.

In passing it may be noted that there are two main sets of constraints on the form of the proposed grammar and that taken together they are very stringent, although the present outline cannot adequately make them obvious. Firstly, the form and content of the base is constrained by our hypothesis concerning the nature of the relationships between language and other psychological abilities, and at the same time by empirical linguistic phenomena, such as those discussed in sections 2 and 3, irrespective of what our hypotheses are. Secondly, because, in order for grammar to operate, segments of base-level strings need to correspond precisely with actual meanings in the lexicon, there are constraints on the form of each lexical entry, the order of entries and the structure of the lexicon as a whole. In short, the production of an actual grammar along the suggested lines would require a far more precise specification of syntactic relationships and lexical meanings than has probably been undertaken in any language so far.

It would seem that the utmost economy of the grammar can be assured only if the lexicon is structured in the way suggested. Strings of base sentoids would be processed syntactically and lexically by being 'passed', again as aimed at in (45c), through the successive strata of the lexicon. The nature of each stratum may be summarized in its respective order as follows:

(51)   Configurations of sentoids (S or S_{not} indicating affirmative or negative) would be evaluated so that logical relationships might become labelled and an incidental reduction in the number of sentoids be thereby achieved. Example of an entry:

S_1 *and* S_2 *and* ... *expect* $[S_2$ *and* $S_{1\,\text{not}}]$

$\rightarrow S_1$ although S_2

(52)   Strings of base VP's will become re-labelled as higher-order stative VP's.
General result of a pass through this stratum:

$$\ldots V_1 \textit{ and } V_1 (\ldots \textit{ and } V_1) \rightarrow \ldots V_2 (\ldots \text{ and } V_1)$$

$V_2 \rightarrow$ beautiful ... animate, born ... intelligent ...
break, burn, move ... (stative meanings only)

(53)   A series of strata, through which 'passing' will have general results as follows:

  i) $[NP_1 \ldots \text{do–so } [NP_1 \ldots V]] \rightarrow [NP_1 \ldots V_1]$

$V_1 \rightarrow \left[\begin{array}{l} \textit{arrive, come, go} \ldots \\ \textit{run, walk} \ldots \end{array} \right]$

  ii) $[NP_1 \ldots \text{do–so } [\ldots N_2 \ldots V]]$

$\rightarrow \left\{ \begin{array}{l} [NP_1 \ldots v_t \; NP_2 \ldots] \; / \; \text{Topicalization of } NP_1 \\ [NP_2 \ldots \text{be-}v_t \quad NP_1 \ldots] \; / \; \text{Topicalization of } NP_2 \end{array} \right\}$

$vt \rightarrow \left[\begin{array}{l} \text{hit, push} \ldots \\ \text{eat, smoke} \ldots \\ \text{elect, choose} \ldots \\ \text{hold, keep, put} \ldots \end{array} \right]$

  iii) $[NP_1 \ldots \text{be–so } [NP_2 \ldots \text{be-v}_{\substack{\text{possess} \\ \text{adv.}}}]]$

$\rightarrow \left\{ \begin{array}{l} [NP_1 \ldots \text{have } NP_2 \ldots] \; / \; \text{Topicalization of } NP_1 \\ [NP_2 \ldots \text{be-prep. } NP_1 \ldots] \; / \; \text{Topicalization of } NP_2 \end{array} \right\}$

iv) $[NP_1 \ldots V_{\text{sensation}}^{} \quad [NP_1 \ldots \underset{V}{\text{be--V}}]]$
$\phantom{iv) [NP_1 \ldots V_{}}$ desideration

$\rightarrow$
$\left\{\begin{array}{l} [NP_1 \ldots \left\{\begin{array}{l} V_{\text{sensation}} \quad \text{Adj} \\ V_{\text{desideration}} \text{ 'to'--Infin.} \end{array}\right\}] \; / \; \text{Topicalization of first occurrence of } NP_1 \\[2em] [NP_1 \ldots \; V_{\text{sensation}} \quad \text{(that)} \quad NP_1 \; \underset{V}{\text{be--v}}] \; / \; \text{Primary} \\ \phantom{[NP_1 \ldots \; V_{}} \text{desideration} \qquad\qquad\qquad\qquad \text{and secondary topicalization respectively of the two occurrences of } NP_1 \end{array}\right.$

(54)　A series of strata, through which 'passing' will result in a labelling of nouns, pronouns (including relatives), and so on, with general results as follows:

At the end of this fourth series of lexical passes, most sentence forms, including the passive voice, and with all the contingent lexis except abstract nouns and nominalizations, would have been generated. It is envisaged that further processes dependent on the form of lexical items, as well as some processes involving rearrangements of syntactic components of sentences, would continue to apply in the grammar to produce all possible items of syntax and lexis, but discussion of these is impossible here. It is hoped, however that the preceding outline is adequate to suggest the general form of the grammar that seems necessary if phenomena of the mind earlier illustrated in the Creole-English continuum are to be accounted for.

In such accounting within the envisaged grammar differentiation between part-of-speech categories would no longer be the barrier it now is to the specification of content relationships between differently structured sentences. Apart from the strictly theoretical significance of this, there are important practical implications that are particularly crucial in continuum and similar situations where inferences about the cognitive and intellectual capacities of differently socialized speakers sometimes tend to be made on the basis of syntactic and lexical characteristics. A whole educational tradition going back to the early 1960s (based on the earlier works of Bernstein and works such as those in the USA criticized in Labov [1970]) which makes inferences from social-class differences in lexis and syntax, has grown up in such situations. In such situations as shown in Craig (1974) for example, procedures of linguistic analysis which permit a principled assessment of the underlying conceptual content of sentences, irrespective of syntactic and lexical variation, are urgently needed.

Note

1. The Creole-language data herein referred to were collected and transcribed by Peter Roberts in the Language Education Research Project funded by the Ford Foundation at the University of the West Indies, Jamaica, and directed by the writer between 1971 and 1975.

References

Alatis, J. (ed.) 1970. *Report of the twentieth annual round table meeting on linguistics and language studies*. Washington, DC: Georgetown University Press.

Bach, E. 1968. "Nouns and noun phrases". In: *Universals in linguistic theory*, ed. by E. Bach and R.T. Harms, pp. 91–122. New York: Holt, Rinehart and Winston, Inc.

Bach, E., and R.T. Harms (eds.) 1968. *Universals in linguistic theory*. New York: Holt Rinehart and Winston, Inc.

Bailey, B. 1966. *Jamaican Creole Syntax*. Cambridge: Cambridge University Press.

Bedell, G. 1974. "The arguments about deep structure". *Language* 50: 423–45.

Bernstein, B. 1961. "Social structure, language and learning". *Educational Research* 3.

Bickerton, D. 1973. "The structure of polylectal grammars". In: *Report of the Twenty-third Annual Round Table Meeting on Linguistics and Language Studies*, ed. by R.W. Shuy, pp. 17–42. Washington, DC: Georgetown University Press.

Bolinger, D.L. 1965. "The atomization of meaning". *Language* 41: 555–73.

Chomsky, N. 1957. *Syntactic Structures*. The Hague: Mouton.

———. 1965. *Aspects of the Theory of Syntax*. Cambridge, MA: MIT Press.

———. 1970. "Remarks on nominalization". In: *Readings in English Transformational Grammar*, ed. by R. Jacobs and P.S. Rosenbaum , pp. 184–221. Waltham, MA: Ginn and Co.

———. 1972. *Studies on Semantics in Generative Grammar*. The Hague: Mouton.

Craig, D. 1974. "Developmental and social class differences in language". *Caribbean Journal of Education* 4 (3): 5–23. University of the West Indies, Jamaica.

Fillmore, C-J. 1968. "The case for case". In: *Universals in Linguistic Theory*, ed. by E. Bach and R.T. Harms, pp. 1–88. New York: Holt, Rinehart and Winston, Inc.

Fraser, B. 1973. "Optional rules in a grammar". In: *Report of the twenty-third annual round table meeting on linguistics and language studies*, ed. by R. W. Shuy, pp. 1–15. Washington, DC: Georgetown University Press.

Hasegawa, K. 1968. "The passive construction in English". *Language* 44: 230–43.

Hymes, D. (ed.) 1971 *Pidginization and Creolization of Languages*. Cambridge: Cambridge University Press.

Jacobs, R., and P.S. Rosenbaum (eds.) 1970. *Readings in English Transformational Grammar*. Waltham, MA: Ginn and Co.

Katz, J., and J. Fodor. 1963. "The structure of a semantic theory". *Language* 39: 170–210.

Labov, W. 1971. "The notion of 'system' in Creole languages". In: *Pidginization and Creolization of Languages*, ed. by D. Hymes, pp. 447–472. Cambridge: Cambridge University Press.

———. "The logic of non-Standard English". In: *Report of the Twenty-third Annual Round Table Meeting on Linguistics and Language Studies*, ed. by J. Alatis, pp. 1–43. Washington, DC: Georgetown University Press.

———. 1973. " Where do grammars stop?" In: *Report of the Twenty-third Annual Round Table Meeting on Linguistics and Language Studies*, ed. by R.W. Shuy, pp. 43–88. Washington, DC: Georgetown University Press.

Lakoff, G. 1970. *Irregularity in Syntax*. New York: Holt, Rinhehart and Winston.

Lakoff, G., and J.R. Ross. 1967. "Is deep structure necessary?" Indian University, Linguistics Club.

McCawley, J.D. 1968. "The role of semantics in grammar". In: *Universals in linguistic Theory*, ed. by E. Bach and R.T. Harms, pp. 124–69. New York: Holt, Rinehart and Winston, Inc.

Ross, J.R. 1969. "Auxiliaries as main verbs". *Journal of Philosophical Linguistics*, Evanston, Illinois.

Schachter, P. 1973. "On syntactic categories". Indiana University, Linguistics Club.

Shuy, R.W. (ed.) 1973. *Report of the Twenty-third Annual Round Table Meeting on Linguistics and Language Studies*. Washington, DC: Georgetown University Press.

8 | Creolistics and Education

Creole-language Situations and Applied Creolistics

The late John E. Reinecke, at the end of his foreword to Valdman (1977: x) in referring to studies of language policy, planning and education in Creole-language situations suggested that they were what he would call "applied creolistics" and that such studies could not but profit from the combined data of precise, descriptive studies, no matter how limited in scope individual samples of that data might be. And such data have been accumulating for a very long time, as DeCamp pointed out:

> Allusions, travelers' accounts, and even fragmentary texts of pidgins date back to the middle ages. Historians in the eighteenth century 'described' the Caribbean creoles. But such early accounts were generally limited to invectives and parodies, providing little information beyond the fact that the author had contempt for the pidgin or creole. In 1868 Russell published the first reliable and extensive account of Jamaican Creole. In 1869 Thomas did the same for the French creole of Trinidad. In the 1880s and 90s there appeared many scholarly accounts of pidgins and creoles from all over the world [. . .] The greatest of these early scholars and the undisputed father of pidgin-creole studies was Hugo Schuchardt (1842–1927). (DeCamp 1971: 30 f.)

Reinecke, writing some seven years later than DeCamp, says essentially the same, but from a different perspective and dominance of interest:

> Creole studies, if we begin with J.M. Magen's Grammatica over det Creolske sprog (1770), have passed their bicentennial. Chronologically speaking, they were by no means in their infancy forty-five years ago. A number of reasonably full descriptions of particular languages had appeared before Schuchardt's time. Beginning with Greenfield's surprisingly sophisticated defence (1830) of the Surinam Negro-English Testament [. . .] and Van Name's survey of eight West Indian creoles (1870), we can detect a movement toward the comparative study of creoles of European lexical base. (Reinecke 1977:vii)

Since Schuchardt, however, and especially since the 1960s, the data that makes an applied creolistics possible have been becoming increasingly systematized in two respects: firstly, through detailed listing and cataloguing of Creole-language situations (for example Hancock 1971, 1977) and of studies of such situations (for example Primus 1972, Reinecke et al. 1975); and secondly through studies which compile or synthesize research findings relating to individual pidgins/Creoles and represent them as constituting a single field (for example Hymes 1971 reflecting the 1960s, Valdman 1977 and Valdman and Highfield 1980 reflecting the 1970s, and an ever increasing volume of texts as, for example, Holm 1988, Mülhaüsler 1986, Rickford 1988, and Thomason and Kaufman 1988, reflecting the 1980s).

This systematization of the data of Creole studies, by bringing together the results achieved by a large number of original researchers, makes it more possible than might otherwise have been the case for applied creolistics to be meaningful and to contribute to the development of these societies that are pidgin/Creole influenced. Language education in such societies is probably the most important aspect of applied creolistics, involving as it does language planning and policy of the society on the one hand and the language related behaviour of Creole-influenced persons on the other.

Relevant Characteristics of Creole-language Situations

Creole-language situations are distinguished by some important general characteristics that have a bearing on education in such situations. One such general characteristic is that monolingual speakers of the Creole tend to be persons of low social status. This is a direct consequence of the fact that, in contact-situations where pidgin/Creole languages originate, first-generation speakers have their prior native language against which the pidgin/Creole can be no more than a second language, that is, a language of convenience. Second generation and subsequent speakers therefore, who find themselves in the position of having only the pidgin/ Creole as their language must be products of low prestige home environments where the preservation of the ancestral first language is not socially advantageous, and where the inheritance of the prestige language from the original contact situation has not been a possibility. This general characteristic may become blurred in continuum situations such as those pertaining in the English lexicon and French-lexicon Creole areas of the Caribbean, where being able to shift along the continuum into a more standard variety of language (which might yet fall short of the fully standard variety) moves the speaker out of the category of being a monolingual Creole speaker.

One consequence of the generally low social status of monolingual Creole speakers is that, unless specific action is taken by the society or the government to make the Creole language equally acceptable with other languages in the formal business of the society, the Creole language will find it difficult to gain acceptance as a national language. Since the 1970s, instances of explicit governmental action to institute Creoles as national languages can be seen in Haiti (cf. Valdman 1980) and New Guinea (cf. Wurm 1977), for example.

A second important characteristic of Creole language situations is a very strong relationship between language and culture. It is true that all languages have a relationship to the culture of their speakers, but in Creole language situations, the relationship assumes overwhelming significance because of the relative newness of Creole or Creole-influenced society. Present-day Creole societies, emerging out of the intensified contacts between different peoples that occurred in the seventeenth and eighteenth centuries, have unique features derived from and associated with their physical environments on the one hand, and the mixing of their preceding ancestral cultures on the other. These unique features find their strongest assertion in the language of the ordinary people, and reflect the varied circumstances of their way of life. This explains why issues that have to do with the instrumentalization of Creole languages have been so heatedly debated in most parts of the world where monolingual Creole speakers exist in appreciable numbers. Devonish (1986) for example sees such issues as being concerned with fundamental human rights and the liberation of oppressed peoples, and gives a comprehensive account of the debate in the Caribbean. The recognition, among Creole speakers themselves, of this strong link between their language and the unique aspects of their culture can sometimes produce attitudes of hostility and rejection of official language policies that concern education. This factor will be noticed subsequently when educational programmes are being considered.

A third general characteristic of Creole languages that has a bearing on education is their similarity in structural form, and the way how this structural form differentiates them from the world's international languages. This characteristic of Creole has been much commented upon. The fact that the similarity exists has led scholars to seek a common origin for Creole languages. The earliest suggestion concerning such as an origin is the monogenetic theory; that the original speakers, at least of the Atlantic Creoles, developed their language from a previous Portuguese-based pidgin that was prevalent along the West African coast (cf. Thompson 1961, Taylor 1961, Stewart 1962, Whinnom 1965, DeCamp 1971: 18–25 and Todd 1974: 32–42). Another version of the monogenetic theory, Afrogenesis, developed by Richard Allsopp 1976 and later revised in 2004 for the Society for Caribbean Linguistics, suggests that the original source of the structural similarity of Creole languages is not a previous pidgin of any kind, but West African languages themselves (cf. Allsopp 1976, 1977). The common characteristic of monogenetic theories of both types is that they attempt to account for the salient features of the Creole languages by reference to one of the substrate languages that can be inferred to have entered into the formation of Creoles. Alleyne (1980) sees the issue essentially in terms of bilingual contact and language shift.

In opposition to theories of monogenesis are universalist theories about the formation of Creoles. The latter theories suggest that there are universal characteristics inherent in human beings that will induce them to develop the same kind of language if they are placed in contact situations anywhere in the world. Different emphases are apparent in different versions of universalist theories, and some of these emphases are more relevant to education than others are, although as a whole universalist, rather than substrate theories, are the ones that seem to hold most implications for education. Bickerton (1981) for example proposes that there is an innate bioprogramme common to all humans, and that apart from Creoles, this bioprogramme is evident only in child language; Anderson (1983) sees universal aspects of pidginization and creolization in terms of language acquisition; and Slobin (1979) sees them in terms of linguistic processing strategies and the inevitable requirements for the use of language.

But these proposals concerning the implications of Creole language structure, do not seem to go far enough towards approaching a unified account of what seem to be closely related phenomena.

The present writer has been seeking such a unified account (Craig 1971, and subsequently 1980, 1984, 1988) suggesting:

(a) that the characteristic structural features of Creole predispose Creole speakers towards a particular style or format of communication, which is different from that of the dominant (European) substrate;

(b) that in continuum situations, the ability of speakers to process simultaneously the grammars of both Creole and substrate suggests an abstract grammatical base which is, in effect, a representation of the structure of cognition; and

(c) that a representation of the structure of cognition, together with a specification of the possible strategies that are available to the human begin for communicating cognition, would jointly provide an explanation for the form of child language, the form of Creole and the relationship between these and what Bickerton (1981) refers to as social languages.

From this it can be seen that the similarity of Creoles in their linguistic structure, and the specific nature of that similarity, have possible implications not only for our understanding of the origin of Creoles, but also for our accounting for child language, certain fundamental universals in language generally, and eventually for the education of Creole-speaking children.

The Conditioning of Children in Creole-language Situations

The three kinds of characteristics common to Creole-language situations, and the possible implications of these characteristics, result in the fact that Creole-speaking children or, no less so, Creole-influenced children who are in situations of decreolization, come into formal education after experiencing a conditioning process which needs to be carefully understood by educators. Extensive discussion of this conditioning has been given in Craig (1971, 1976, 1977), but some of what has been said, particularly in Craig (1977) bears some repetition here:

> Continued orality in creole in the primary school means that children become consolidated not merely in the phonological, morphological, and syntactic conventions of creole, but also in the way in which concepts are given lexical form or idiomized in creole. If literacy in creole is also one of the aims of primary

education, then this will strongly reinforce the consolidation, but whether or not literacy in creole is an aim, the acquisition of a standard (and particularly a European standard) second language will manifest the influence of a creole-language style of communication. This is not a matter that can be dismissed as one of the incidentals of first-language interference with the learning of a second language. It is a matter that has to do with the specific cognitive orientations of individuals, and that is known to be important for education even in language situations where difference between speakers are of the social-dialect kind, rather than of the type between more disparate language systems. (Craig 1977: 325)

Apart from the preceding, Creole-speaking or Creole-influenced children are likely to be affected by social-class factors. Creole-language situations, as remarked earlier, are invariably situations of lower-social-class status, and especially where a continuum has developed between a Creole and a standard language, as in the English-official Caribbean, the structure of socio-cultural linguistic differences is not unlike those noticed in metropolitan countries between social-class extremes. It was such differences that led Bernstein (1962a, b) to propose the theory of restricted and elaborated codes and Labov (1969), subsequently to counter with his analysis of the logic of non-Standard English. Since then, apart from a general acceptance in education that there is value to be derived from the early intellectual stimulation of children, the study of social-class linguistic differences has led to the general conclusion that differences are just that- differences, and they signify no absolute superiority or inferiority in one set of speakers rather than in another.

But this conclusion, though probably demonstrable in purely pragmatic terms, cannot be logically explained without an explanation of how different sets of linguistic elements can function as alternative in the communication of a common cognitive or experiential content. Craig (1984) summarizes an approach to such an explanation in terms of contrasting communication styles which permit speakers to perform fully equivalent cognitive operations on the same given subject matter; it is further suggested that each communication style has its advantages for special purposes, but that neither is absolutely superior to the other.

The significance of this for an assessment of the psycholinguistic conditioning of the Creole-speaking or Creole-influenced child is commented upon in Craig (1977) as follows:

> It seems that primary education in all types of creole-language contexts would be subject in different ways to the effects of communication differences such as those

referred to; and, unless the nature of such differences is understood, educators in creole-language contexts might be led into unfounded assumptions similar to those that underlie theories of cultural and linguistic deprivation. The fact that communication differences of the relevant kind appear not only between the European-based creoles and their respective standard languages, but also between other creole languages and their standard languages, points to the universality of the danger. Heine (1975), for example, points out that African-based pidgin-creoles (like the Swahili and Zulu pidgins, for example) have the following universal characteristics relative to their respective standard African languages:

(a) lower type-token ratios;
(b) suppression of redundant distinctions of number and gender;
(c) fewer non-class distinctions;
(d) fewer distinctions of tense and modality;
(e) fewer complex sentences and fewer markers of types of embedding;
(f) more conjoining as a means of linking sentences.

There is striking similarity between these characteristics and those of the Bernstein restricted code relative to the elaborated code, non-Standard English relative to Standard English, and European-based Creoles relative to their standard languages; the implications for primary education in all cases seem to be exactly the same. (Craig 1977: 326 f.).

Education Policies and their Determinants

The common characteristics of Creole language which have been outlined, and the way in which children are conditioned psycholinguistically by those characteristics, determine the teaching strategies or methodologies that will be appropriate in classrooms for various purposes.

If, for example, a teacher wants to teach initial reading in English to a child whose home language is an English-based Creole such as Krio, or Guyanese, or Jamaican or Hawaiian, because of the conditioning the child would already have received, the teacher would need to do the following:

(a) teach the child the vocabulary of the immediate reading material – if that vocabulary is not already possessed by the child;
(b) teach the child to use orally such structures of English as will be necessary for understanding the reading material.

The teacher may use a variety of methods to achieve (a) and (b) either singly or jointly, but the point is that the teacher's activity would have to be guided in any case by the teacher's understanding of the characteristics of Creole and how the child has been conditioned by those characteristics.

Prior to the teacher's activity, however, someone would have had to arrive at a decision that initial reading must be taught in English. This decision could have been justified, like the teacher's activity, in terms of the language situation and the previous conditioning of the child. The point is, however, that this kind of decision does not need to be justified at the level of language policy, and the teacher would have had to implement the decision in any case, irrespective of the specific characteristics of Creole and the conditioning received by the child, although the latter factors could make the policy decision more difficult or less difficult to implement. Policy decisions could be based ultimately on factors which, in whole or part, might have no bearing or dependence on factors of the Creole language or in the conditioning of speakers.

Factors which determine language policy have been considered from two aspects. One of these is to be seen in Carrington (1976). Carrington's proposals are summarized and commented upon in Craig (1980), as follows:

> Carrington (1976) has already suggested that the following considerations; linguistic relationship between the popular and the official language, the degree to which a continuum is present, the identifiability or a norm acceptable to the population, the level of national consciousness, and the geographical and age distribution of languages determine what should be the language of instruction in schools. From these considerations, Carrington (1976) derives six principles which may be applied to determine whether a language other than the official language of a territory should be used as a medium of instruction. However, by limiting its discussion merely to the question of a medium of instruction, Carrington (1976) does not manage to discuss alternative education policy models [. . .]. (Craig 1980b: 253–55)

The aspect involving alternative education policy models is the second aspect from which factors that determine education policy have been considered, and this is done in Craig (1980) where the five models of bilingual education proposed in Fishman and Lovas (1970): school monolingualism in the dominant language, transitional bilingualism, monoliterate bilingualism, partial bilingualism and full bilingualism are shown to be each selectable in Creole-language situations, depending on the specific configuration of two sets of determining factors, which are outlined as follows in Craig (1980b):

The first set of these factors is the purely linguistic one that has to do with questions such as the following:

- Whether there is a lexical or structural relationship between the creole and the more dominant language with which it coexists.
- Whether there are languages additional to the creole and the dominant language in the particular situation and, if there are, whether specific roles are attached to each.
- Whether phenomena such as diglossia or a continuum, indicating functional interchange or alternation have developed.

It is the linguistic factor, for example, that makes it easier, all other factors remaining unconsidered at the moment, for the status-quo model in many creole communities to be school monolingualism in the dominant language where there is a lexical or structural relationship or a continuum between that language and the creole. On the other hand, however, in a situation where there is no relationship between the creole and the dominant language or where mutual intelligibility practically negates such a relationship, the status quo, in the absences of planning, is more likely to be transitional bilingualism.

The second set of factors that could enter into the determining of a policy model has to do with the socio-economic and cultural characteristics of the whole society in which the creole speech community exists. This set could possibly be sub-categorized into several discrete components, but for the sake of simplicity it is treated here as a unity. It has to do with questions such as the following:

- Whether the creole language is a strong element in a particular subculture and tradition.
- Whether the population strength or socio-economic strength of the creole subculture and tradition is significant within the national context, and if it is, at what level.
- Whether the society is stratified in terms of social class, race or colour and, if it is, what is the more prevalent status of the creole speech community within such stratification.
- Whether the creole language and subculture is viewed with acceptance or rejection by the rest of the society.

It is the balance within this set of socio-cultural factors, including language attitudes as it does, that stimulates, or inhibits, in any society, the decision as to whether, in respect of creole-speakers, there is to be any educational policy going beyond school monolingualism in the dominant language or merely transitional bilingualism. Unless, within this set of factors, there is a positive balance that favours the retention or preservation or Creole, there will tend to be no conscious planning and no selection of an educational policy other than one or other of the first two models (school monolingualism or transitional bilingualism) into which it is possible for societies merely to drift, as pointed out already. (Craig 1980: 252 f.).

Teaching the Standard in Decreolized Situations

The education policy alternatives that have been proposed for Creole language situations all envisage that at some stage of education, an attempt will be made to teach a standard international language to Creole-speaking or Creole-influenced speakers. In many situations of decreolization, where a language continuum (cf. Rickford 1987: 15–40) invariably exists, it is Creole-influenced speakers, rather than full Creole-speaking speakers, who will have to be catered for in related standard-language teaching.

In Craig (1976, 1983) it is shown that in the latter situations, because of learners' high ability to recognize the related target standard, while learners' production ability remains low, neither native-language nor foreign-language teaching methods can be efficacious, and a distinctively different methodology (which has been described since the 1960s) has to be adopted.

The need for this distinctive methodology in teaching a related standard language to Creole-influenced speakers in continuum situations still needs to be stressed, however, especially in the context of the latest fashions in foreign and second-language teaching which tend towards a reliance on communicative methodologies (cf. Brumfit 1984). The fact is that Creole-influenced learners of a related standard language can communicate effectively in any standard-language situation, and be completely unaware of whether their language production in that situation is standard or Creole-influenced. In this situation, it is futile to rely on communicative methodologies if the aim is accuracy – which is what it is in this case.

Conclusion

The preceding has outlined the information necessary to show that in Creole or Creole-influenced language situations, education has to make use of applied creolistics in order to specify those features of Creole situations which provide a psycholinguistic conditioning for persons. This conditioning has to be strongly taken into account in all classroom activity of schools, even though it can possibly be ignored in the determination of language policy at a macro-level.

Since the early 1970s, when much of the information started to become available, the concern over educational provision for linguistic minorities (including Creole speakers) reached a climax that now seems to have subsided. In the Caribbean (English-based) and the USA (non-standard/ decreolization), there were more educational programmes specifically for Creole-influenced speakers in the 1970s than there have been in the 1980s (cf. Taylor et al. 1983), and the teaching of Standard English to such speakers remains as problematical as it has always been in the context where available information that might ameliorate the situation has not been acted upon and reflected in adequate educational materials. In Haiti, the use of Creole in primary education, foreseen in Valdman (1980), continues haltingly in the context of economic and political difficulties in the country and the continuing recognition of the value of an international language, which Creole is not. Almost the same can be said, except for their more stable primary school programmes in several parts of the French-dominated areas (e.g. Seychelles, Guadeloupe) and French-influenced regions (e.g. St Lucia, Dominica), and in the Dutch-influenced Caribbean (Curaçao, Aruba, Surinam) where, having been started, programmes have either ceased or continue in a low key through inadequate support.

The truth is that the movements for the use of Creoles and minority languages that were generally strong in the 1960s and 1970s sprang from ideologies which now seem to have receded and given place in the 1980s to a new internationalism which is being experienced in many respects, not the least of them being an increased recognition of the value of bi- and multi-lingualism, and the need for minority speakers to acquire standard languages (without detriment to their inherited home language).

In this context, information such as that outlined here about creolistics in relation to education seems valuable, not for a narrower purpose such as, for example, literacy in Creole, but for ensuring that the wider education of the Creole-speaking or Creole-influenced person would not suffer by failing to give account of the person's psycholinguistic background, and the alternatives of education policy that are possible.

References

Alatis, J., ed. (1969), *Twentieth Annual Roundtable Meeting,* 22, Georgetown University School of Language and Linguistics.

Alleyne, Mervyn (1980), *Comparative Afro-American.* Ann Arbor: Karoma.

Allsopp, Richard (1976), "The case for Afrogenesis", in Cave (1976).

———. (1977), "Africanisms in the idiom of Caribbean English", in Kotey and Der-Houssikian (1976), 424–41.

Anderson, R. (1983), *Pidginization and Creolization as Language Acquisition,* Rowley, MA: Newbury House.

Bernstein, Basil (1962a), "Linguistic codes, hesitation phenomena and intelligence", *Language and Speech* 5, 31–46.

———. (1962b), "Social class, linguistic codes, and grammatical elements", *Language and Speech* 5, 221–24.

Bickerton, Derek (1981), *Roots of Language,* Ann Arbor: Karoma.

Brumfit, C.J. (1984), *Communicative Methodology in Language Teaching,* London: Cambridge University Press.

Carrington, Lawerence (1976), "Determining language education policy in Caribbean sociolinguistic complexes". *International Journal of the Sociology of Language* 8, 27–4.

Cave, G., ed. (1976), *New Directions in Creole Studies: Papers Presented at the Annual Conference of the Society for Caribbean Linguistics,* Georgetown, Guyana: Library, University of Guyana.

Craig, Dennis (1971), Education and Creole English in the West Indies: Some sociolinguistic factors", in Hymes (1971), 371–91

———. (1976), "Bidialectal education: Creole and Standard in the West Indies", *International Journal of the Sociology of Language* 8, 93–114.

———. (1977), "Creole languages and primary education", in Valdman (1977), 313–32.

———. (1980a), "A Creole English continuum and the theory of grammar", in Day (1980), 113–31.

———. (1980b), "Models for educational policy in Creole-speaking communities", in Valdman and Highfield (1980), 245–66.

———. (1983), "Teaching Standard English to non-Standard speakers: Some methodological issues", *Journal of Negro Education* 52, Washington: Howard University Press, 65–74.

———. (1984), "Communication, Creole and conceptualization", *International Journal of the Sociology of Language* 45, 21–37.

———. (1988), "Cognition and situational context: Explanations from English lexicon Creole", *International Journal of the Sociology of Language* 71, 11–23.

Day, Richard, ed. (1980), *Issues in English Creoles,* VEAW 2, Heidelberg: Groos.

DeCamp, David (1971), "The study of pidgin and creole languages", in Hymes (1971), 13–39.

Devonish, Hubert (1986), *Language and Liberation,* London: Karia.

Fishman, Joshua A. (1968), *Readings in the Sociology of Language,* The Hague: Mouton.

——— and J. Lovas (1970), "Bilingual education in sociolinguistic perspective", *TESOL Quarterly* 4, 215–22.

Hancock, Ian (1971), "A map and list of pidgin and creole languages", in Hymes (1971), 509–24.

Heine, Bernd (1975),"Some generalizations on African-based pidgins", International Conference on Pidgins and Creoles, University of Hawaii.

Holm, John (1988), *Pidgin and Creoles: Theory and Structure,* vol. 1. Cambridge: Cambridge University Press.

Hymes, Dell, ed. (1971), *Pidginization and Creolization of Languages,* Cambridge: Cambridge University Press.

Kotey, P. and H. Der-Houssikian (1976), *Language and Lingusitic Problems in Africa,* South Carolina: Hornbeam.

Labov, W. (1969), "The logic of non-Standard English", in Alatis (1969).

Le Page, R.B., ed. (1961), *Creole Language Studies 2,* London: Macmillan.

Mühlhaüsler, Peter (1986), *Pidgin and Creole Linguistics,* Oxford: Blackwell.

Primus, Wilma J. (1972), *Creole and Pidgin Languages in the Caribbean: A Select Bibliography,* UNESCO/UWI Conference on Creole Languages and Educational Development, St Augustine, Trinidad: Library/University of the West Indies.

Reinecke, John E., Stanley M. Tsuzaki, David DeCamp, Ian F. Hanckock and Richard E. Wood, eds., *A Bibliography of Pidgin and Creole Languages,* Honolulu: University of Hawaii Press.

Reinecke, John E., ed., in collaboration with David DeCamp, Ian F. Hancock, Stanley Tsuzaki, Richard Wood (1977), "A bibliography of pidgin and creole linguistics" (Oceanic Linguistics Special Publication, no. 14). *Language in Society* 6(3), 429–33.

Rice, F.A. (1962), *Study of the Role of Second Languages in Asia, Africa, and Latin America,* Washington, DC: Center for Applied Linguistics.

Rickford, John R. (1987), *Dimensions of a Creole Continuum,* Stanford: Stanford University Press.

———, ed.(1988), *Sociolinguistics and Pigin and Creole Studies.* International Journal of the Sociology of Language 71, Berlin: de Gruyter.

Slobin, D. (1979), *Psycholinguistics,* Glenview, IL: Scott, Foresman.

Stewart, W.A. (1962). "Creole languages in the Caribbean". In Rice (1962), 34–53.

Taylor, Douglas (1961), "New languages for old in the West Indies: Comparative studies in society and history", in Fishman (1968), 607–19.

Taylor, Orlando, K. Payne and P. Cole (1983), "A survey of bidialectical language arts programs in the United States", *Journal of Negro Education* 52, 35–45.

Thomason, Sarah Grey, and Terrence Kauffman (1988), *Language Contact, Creolization and Genetic Linguistics*, Berkeley: University of California Press.

Thompson, R. (1961), "A note on some possiblie affirmities between the creole dialects of the Old World and those of the New", in Le Page (1961), 107–13.

Todd, Loreto (1974), *Pidgins and Creoles*, London: Routledge and Kegan Paul.

Valdman, Albert, ed. (1977), *Pidgins and Creole Linguistics,* Bloomington: Indiana University Press.

—— and A. Highfield, eds. (1980), *Theoretical Orientations in Creole Studies*, New York: Academic Press.

—— and I. Joseph (1980), *Créole enseignement primaire en Haiti,* Bloomington: Indiana University Press.

Whinnom, Keith. 1965. "The origin of European-based creoles and pidgins", *Orbis* 14, 509–27.

Wurm, S.A. 1977. Pidgins, creoles and lingua francae, and national development", in Valdman (1977), 333–57.

Notes on the Editors

Jeannette Allsopp, now retired, was Senior Research Fellow in Lexicography, Director of the Centre for Caribbean Lexicography, English and Multilingual, and Lecturer in Linguistics, University of the West Indies Cave Hill, Barbados. Her many publications include the *French-Spanish Supplement* to the *Dictionary of Caribbean English Usage* by Richard Allsopp, the *Caribbean Multilingual Dictionary of Flora, Fauna and Foods,* and *Language, Culture and Caribbean Identity* (co-edited with John R. Rickford).

Zellynne Jennings, now retired, was Professor of Curriculum Development and Director of the School of Education, University of the West Indies, Mona, Jamaica, and former Professor of Education, University of Guyana. She is the author of several reading texts for primary schools and of *Labba and Creek Water: Stories from the Caribbean.* She is the widow of Dennis Craig.

www.ingramcontent.com/pod-product-compliance
Lightning Source LLC
Chambersburg PA
CBHW020704270326
41928CB00005B/264